Americas
and
Other Places

Americas
and
Other Places

G.B. Ryan

ELKHOUND
NEW YORK

For Stephanie, Peter and Lincoln

For Louis

For Norma

Copyright © 2013 G.B Ryan. All rights reserved.

ISBN: 978-0-615-79729-8

Contact G.B. Ryan at ryangb2@gmail.com

Printed and bound by Thomson-Shore, Inc.
7300 West Joy Road, Dexter, MI 48130
www.thomsonshore.com

Elkhound Publications
Gracie Station Box 1453
New York, NY 10028
elkhound460@gmail.com

CONTENTS

New York

1
Bryant Park, 1
Woman Speaking on Bus, 1
Eagle, 1
Late Afternoon, 2
Afternoon, Central Park, 2
Bells, 2
Autumn, 3
Deal, 3
Nocturne, from a Window, 4
Your Right Nipple, 4
Central Park, Early March, 5
Rooftop Lullaby, 5
Gulls, 5
A Name, 6
Interrupted by Dawn, 7
Wasp, 7
The Lady in the Lake, 8
A Visitor?, 8
In a Midtown Post Office, 9

2
Sunday Evening, July, 10
Early Lunch, 11
Takeover, 13
Bank of Elevators, 14
Heat, Vistas, the Source, Pacific, 14
Rooftop, 15
April Again, 15
Jones Beach, September, 16
Bus Stop, January, 16
111 Mott Street, 17
Bag In Tree, 17
Frontier Life, 18
Photo of 19th Century Dignitaries, 18
New York City, 1904, 29

3
Midtown Ecology, 20
She Thinks Back, 20
Near Rhinebeck, 21
Photos from Space, 21
Unseen Passenger, 22
Signals, 23
Nude, 24
War Cry, 24
Christmas on Third Avenue, 24
Tapeworm, 25
Ramadan, 25
Ark, 26
Mourning Dove, 26
Message Received, 27
A Visitor by Night, 28
A Warm Evening, 28
Thief, 29
Bouquet, 30
Three Dialogues, 30
Linden, 32
Grass and Stuff, 32
Who Has Woken?, 33
Twitch, 33
Out There, 34
Interrupted Call, 35
A Landmark Gone, 36
Last Wish, 36
A Sight to See, 37
Halloween, 37
Get Yourself a Dog, 38
Ill Wind, 38

4
Hospital Floor, 39
View, 39
Independence Day on the Hudson River, 40
Me and the Mob, 41
Warning Geese, 42
Style, 42
Woman with a Question, 43
Goethe House Recital, 44
On the Side of a Building, 45
Spring, 45
Three Storm Warnings, 45
Banner and Drums, 46
Taxi on Lexington, 47

Good Morning, 48
Unidentified Saint, 49
Only a Wavelength Away, 49
Westward, 50
On the Way Up, 51
A Ferrari, 52
Enlarged Detail, 53
First Anniversary of Twin Towers, 53
Why Are You Walking?, 54
Shower, 55
Live Performance, 55
Quandary, 56
It Can't Be Here, 56
Obituary, 57
A Drive in the Country, 58
Francois, 59
Ask Not, 59
Greenwood Men, 60
I Hate to Say It, 61
On 10th Street, 61
Thinking of Home, 62

5
Subway Passenger, 63
On Their Way, 63
Not This Relic, 64
Encounter, 64
Crossing a Street, 65
Hudson River Solitaire, Near Rhinecliff, 65
Label, 66
Comfort Shopping, 66
No Sixpack, 67
Outside a Building, 67
A Detail from Reality, 68
Waiting to Cross the Street, 68
Joke as Poem, 69
The Dark Side, 69
What Can We Do?, 69
Subway Foam, 70
Cawk Spoke Squawk, 70
A God Offended, 71
Star Trek Encounter, 72
Weaving Car, 73
Singing Woman, 74

6

Hour of Departure, 75
Construction Supervisors, 75
Inward Eye, 76
Conjuror, 76
Migrating Butterfly, 77
Supermarket Incident, 77
Memorial at First and 49th, 77
Patient Break, 78
Couples, 78
Telephones, 80
A Lesson in Pricing, 80
Generations, 81
In a Crosstown Bus, 81
In Brooklyn, 82
By the Wayside, 83
Advice to the Police Academy, 84
Pedestrian Crossing, 85
Knock on This Door, 86
November, 86
Sweet Assassin, 87
Sorting Mail, 88
Response, 88

7

A New Mythology, 89
Like It Is, 90
Underground, 90
Surprised by Gulls, 91
Throwing Out a Bookcase, 92
Late Afternoon, First and 88th, 93
Limousine Drivers, 94
Art Collection, 94
Girl in Art Museum, 95
Street Art, 95
April Is Here, 96
Hospital Tomatoes, 96
Changed Times, 97
Try Lourdes, 97
Neighbor, 98
Yoga, 98
Untitled, 99
Thieves, 99
Daybreak, 100
Holiday Pizza, 100
Before Dawn, 101
East River Views, 101

8
Volunteer, 103
New Year Awakening, 103
Radio Timer Accidentally Set, 104
In Passing, 104
Out of Touch, 105
Strange People in Subways, 106
AARP: 99 Great Ways to Save!, 106
Star Performer, 107
Headline, 107
Suspicion, 108

Americas

1
Christmas, 109
From Webster's Third New International Dictionary, 109
Push, 110
Blue Sky, 110
The Semidomesticated, 110
Astronaut in the Afternoon, 111
Leaves, 112
Silent Wood, 112
Real-World Scene, 113
The Witch and Daffodil, 113
Five Miniatures, 115
Nocturne, 116
New England Graveyard Invaded by Trees, 116
Snowscape, 117
Peaceable Kingdom, 117
Equinox, 118
Old People Wandering, 118
To My Daughter, 118
Newlyweds, 119
You Canoe, 119
Afloat, 120
Pissarro in Massachusetts, 121
Stanley Kunitz Gardening, 122
Winter Field, 122
Tour, 123
Photo Opportunity, 123

2

Savannah in July, 124
Headstones with an Irish Name, 124
Alligator, 125
Egrets, 125
Hothouse Geraniums, 126
Distant Funnel, 126
Portavant Indian Mound, 127
Jeff Climbs Out and Walks Away, 127
Alabama, 1964, 128
Perennial Weed, 129
Eastern Shore, 129

3

Indian Guide, 130
His Uncle, 131
Family Visit, 132
Lake Shore, 133
Honeybees Walk, 133
Phantom Infant, 134
Mariner Lost, 134
Need, 135
Walk, 135
Crawl, 136
A Slight Edge, 136
Moons, 137
Say It with Flowers, 138
Pen Name, 138
Her Walk, 139
Early Morning Baudelaire, 139
Clouds, 140
Lancaster County Put-Down, 140
Going Back, 141
Looking for Walter, 141

4

Before Intercontinental Missiles, 142
Ruby Beach, 143
Impression, 143
Friday, 144
Urban Problem, 144
Ponderosa, 145
Elephant Seals in California, 145
Home and Castle, 146
They Hunt to Eat, 147
Bodyguard, 147

Took a Look, 148
Rapper Gunned Down at Upscale Mall, 148
Delta Flight 708, 149
Mandatory Evacuation at 3 a.m., 150
The Los Angeles Basin Story, 151
Quake, 151
Pinkelponkers, 152
Caminito Bravura, 153
Coyote, 153
In Search of Polygamists, 154
Protest, 155
Arizona Afternoon, 155
Mogollon Rim, 156
An Anthropologist Comes Full Circle, 157
In Gallup, 158
La Jungla, 159
Lone Swimmer, 160

Bits and Pieces

Dogs, 161
Insects, 162
Cats, 164
Birds, 167
Ultraviolet Light from Young Stars, 170
Almost Still Lifes, 172
Children, 173
Biz People, 177
It's All Real, 178
USA OK, 179
Ten Poems, 181

Ireland

1
1867: Last Sounds, 184
Schoolroom Incident, 184
Dryad, 184
Moving Parts, 185
Cells, 186
Rain, 187
Fear of Vikings, 187
There and Then, 187
From Another Time, 188
Irish Landscape with Figures, 189
Song, 189

2

A Galway Standoff, 190
Bedside Visitor, 191
One of the Old School, 192
River Teeth, 192
Air Show, 193
An Ancient Irish Saint's Farewell, 193
A Question, 194
Pilgrims, 194
Sibyl, 195
Explanation, 195
High Noon, 195
Thin Air, 197
Two Sayings of Malachy, 198
The One Unreviled, 198
Donore, 199
Three Songs for Tin Whistle, 200

3

Shaping Up the Garden, 201
Seapoint, Dublin, 202
Becoming Ninety, 203
A Generation More, 203
Sisters, 203
Delusion, 204
Her Last Day, 204
From Beyond, 205

4

In the Eye of the Beholder, 206
Out of Season, 206
Dog and Swallow, 207
Down at the Bog, 207
Grace and Rainier, 208
Bed and Breakfast, 208
Traders Now, 209
Old Priest, 210
Dead Fishermen, 210
Teltown Marriage, 211
Glenbuck, County Antrim, 212
Weatherwise, 212
Outside an Irish Country House, 213
Out of This World, 213
At Moll's Gap, in Kerry, 214
Summer Afternoon in Kerry, 215
Peitreal, 215

5
Secure Ward, 216
Trophies, 217
Silencing the Man Who Knew More than Anyone, 218
Dubln Bus Stop, 219
Another Dublin Bus Stop, 219
Monk, 220
Prayer for Niall A., 220
Dean's Grange, 220
Not Lost, 221

6
Lord of the Yard, 222
Plowshares into Swords, 222
Dublin Halloween Long Gone, 223
Warrior, Age Thirteen, 224
Chant, 225
Blue-Winged Olive, 226

Other Places
Warrior, 227
Country Life, 228
A Shard in Somerset, 229
St. Ives, 230
Whispering Leaves, 230
At a Fence, 231
Their New House, 231
Patricia, 232
At an Early Hour, 232
Winner, 233
Ghostly Footsteps in London, 233
Blues and Royals, 234
Ceremonial Duty, 235
Brompton Cemetery, 235
Highgate Cemetery, 235
Noordoostpolder, 236
Norsk Foto, 236
Thunder Outside Moscow, 237
This Way Out, 237
Beasts, 238
Lizard King, 238
The Forest at Night, 239
Aroma, 239
Crusader, 240
Arles Parking Garage, 240

Snails, 240
Think of Flowers, 241
Island, 241
Sketches of Spain in the 1950s, 241
Home Furnishings, 243
Dining Out, 243
After Fernando Pessoa, 244
After Martial, 246
At Night in Arezzo, 247
Peloponnese, 248
Blue, 249
In Crete, 249
Desert Homecoming, 250

No Willows
An Old Story, 251
No Plum Blossoms, 252
Brothers, 254
Homecoming from War, 255
No Chrysanthemums, 256
After Poets of the Late T`ang, 257
No Willows, 258

New York

1

BRYANT PARK

Piston backfires
a car on 42nd Street
and the pigeons lift in a flock
    and wheel away
in ancestral fear of gunfire
although these New York City birds
have never had to dodge the gun.

When shots are real
the barrel is not aimed at them.

WOMAN SPEAKING ON BUS

Now anytime I want to visit him
I just take the Eighth Avenue subway.
It takes only twenty minutes or so,
    twenty or thirty,
and right where I come up the subway steps
    there's a little gate
and there he is, under a lovely tree.

EAGLE

If the moth with things on its antennae
to jam bat-radar ultrasonic cries
had offensive weapons too

instead of being pinned through the middle
in a specimen case
that moth might be the national bird today

LATE AFTERNOON

Air bubbles burst in the aquarium,
an electric pump, a miniature,
hums in the background.
She is breathing deeply in her sleep.

    Marijuana tall
        in the window box,
   the generous plants
        have promising buds.

Her mouth hangs open and her eyes are closed.
I'll let her rest on the couch, without disturbing
the nonchalant pose
in which pleasure surprised her.

AFTERNOON, CENTRAL PARK

the	and	because
senorita	talks	it
feeds	to	is
nuts	it	a
to	in	norte
a	broken	americano
squirrel	English	squirrel

BELLS

The cast-iron sounds bounce down from a Gothic belfry
with that extra bang stone can give to the sound of bells

into the cobblestone square, you might think,
of a town in France on Sunday morning —

but this is Oakland, New Jersey:
the bells sound from a small wooden
building topped by a cupola.

Standing near my car in the supermarket parking lot,
I lift up my eyes and I permit my heart to rejoice:
electronic stereophonic medieval bells.

AUTUMN

Autumn comes to Park Avenue
    a doorman
        picks up the fallen leaf

    DEAL

    An old woman
    opens the door
    of the church

of the Immaculate Conception

    and steps out
    on 14th Street.

Her Mediterranean peasant
face is cracked in gratification.

    Back in the church
    she had struck
    a good bargain.

NOCTURNE, FROM A WINDOW

He opened the yellow Dodge
back door.

She slid in
and he leaned after her.

Kissed goodnight.

Then he withdrew,
closed the taxi door.

And left,
never looked back.

So?

Hard to say,
the way he walked away.

YOUR RIGHT NIPPLE

Your right nipple
reminds
me of the uppermost tip
of a state capitol dome

but your left nipple's different
your left nipple
reminds
me of other nipples

your lips
are the color
of a Macedonian sunset

CENTRAL PARK, EARLY MARCH

A kind woman sprinkles corn for the helicopters,
they're hungry, you can hear their bones rattle in the air,
the chill air — that pierces you through and through, pierces you
to the very bone. The woman kicks at a squirrel.
The rattling bones of helicopters become louder.

ROOFTOP LULLABY

The clouds tiptoe across the afternoon
above a brownstone and an empty lot

a hanging curtain of reflecting glass
that catches them a moment as they pass

the sun skids round a bend on tar and slate
the ventilator pipes begin to spin

no falcon silhouette against the blue
there's nothing in the sky to bother you

GULLS

The East River drains backward with the tide
and here and there a gull wheels, to circle,
dip and hover, investigate a thing
floating submerged in the green dock water,
paper undulating a limb whitely.

Do daddy seagulls eat dead people? No,
little girl, did your mother tell you that?
I suppose not, you thought of it yourself.

Daddy seagulls laugh, they are big and strong,
ah, you can almost smell the ocean breeze
waft in as fresh as aftershave lotion.

A NAME

A small tanker, the *Mary A. Whalen*,
rides high and empty out of the water,
steaming downriver, her red sides peeling.

Who is Mary A.? The captain's mother?

Mary, the shipowner's secretary?
(He's named a supertanker for his wife.)

Whalen? A good Irish name, to be sure.
A nurse perhaps who stood for no nonsense,
a sailor's friend through clap or high fever,
salty Nightingale, all-weather woman.

To call an oil tanker merely *Mary*
without last name or middle initial
dismisses the woman with a lyric,
ideal painted over the real —
the rusty work ships named for a goddess,
nymph, nun, infanta, dowager empress.

Whalen, Mary A., whoever she was,
whenever she lived, that name is real
and of highest sentimental value.

Do not for a moment think that I sneer
at you and your boat, Mary A. Whalen,
an empty tanker with red sides peeling,
as you sail away and I stand ashore
while the gap between us is widening.

That's your monument, this mine. No one wins.

INTERRUPTED BY DAWN

But soft, what light through yonder window breaks?

It is the East. Had we but wings to fly
we could scorn the danger and tarry here,
you and I, wild in love's sweet abandon.

It's a working day, middle of the week,
soon the clock will ring and the bed will creak,
in less than an hour he will be awake.

While he heats the coffee upon the stove,
runs, slaps and tries to figure where in hell
are all these baby roaches coming from,
we'll nestle beneath the linoleum.

WASP

Sun came through the fifteen panes
        of air-clear glass
in an old-fashioned window.

A wasp inside was buzzing
        against the glass.

Had it been a butterfly
        I could have caught
and released it out-of-doors.

But black and yellow banded
        insects can sting.

Gauze calipers could have held
        the panicked beast
without damaging its wings.

Salvation is not sure for
those who look like they can sting.

THE LADY IN THE LAKE

A car parked under a flowering tree
with a Japanese lake in its windshield.

The driver's face shimmers from deep beneath,
her frightened countenance swims in my gaze.

I reach my hand to her. The engine starts.

A VISITOR?

Although the shower curtains are getting old
the wings of the butterflies have not faded
in their mock hygienic shades of green and blue
among white flowers on translucent plastic
that's nearly rigid, perished by steam and age.

The midnight oil flickers in a naked bulb
on a cord from the ceiling, a bright bathroom,
sanctuary for thought and meditation.

The butterflies waver as a curtain moves
and no doubt because I am alone my heart
skips a beat and I wonder is there something
there behind that curtain or is it only
dry arthritic folds of plastic subsiding.

A phenomenon of polymer science?

Or has a dear departed former tenant
returned to his or her beloved shower?

One of the curtains is really moving –
it could be plastic readjusting itself
but the movement seems overelaborate,
a slow billowing and a quick contraction
with much deliberate rippling and curling,
folds crackling, curtains scraping against the tub.

I wait in silence for them to draw apart ...

IN A MIDTOWN POST OFFICE

You write an airmail letter.

You are thin and very pale
and your clothes are worn but clean.

Now you finish the letter.

Your face is bland, it tells me
nothing, not a single thing.

An impersonal letter,
one that gives nothing away?

And back in the Old Country
do they remember you still?

The one who went to America ...

2

SUNDAY EVENING, JULY

A wind turns the paler underside of leaves,
the trees shimmer in waves of moving facets.

      The weekend crowd
load bicycles on cars to drive back to the city.

A watching girl about ten tells them she has never
      been to New York.

      Her father is
an army strongman, a tough balding paratrooper

who lives nearby, proud to be free of the contagion
      of urban blight,

      a hive alive
with scrapers, shredders, collectors and detritivores,

he has told me gravely over scotch and beer chaser
      in a tavern.

      But his daughter
watches them loading their shining ten-speed bicycles

and her expression is one of determination
      mixed with envy.

      She too would own
a French racing bicycle if only *she* lived there.

She is blonde, already pretty, unafraid to speak
      to the people

      from Manhattan,
so far from her hometown bumblebee economy.

EARLY LUNCH

This was when I worked in publishing,
twenty-somethingth floor, Sixth Avenue,
Rockefeller Center, tall buildings
shoulder to shoulder. I worked in
one of many identical
cubicles on one of many
identical floors, business suit, tie,
daily expecting to be replaced.

One early lunch I had too much
whiskey in Hurley's convenient bar
on an empty stomach, didn't eat,
came back to my desk to look at the Times
job ads and geopolitical scene,
only to find I was too late —
the revolution had taken place,
I was overthrown, dispossessed,
some upstart had taken my job,
had lost no time in putting his things
on the shelves in my office, my desk:
pens, folders, neat stacks of documents,
a framed photo of wife and children.

What had happened to my wilderness
of manuscripts and unanswered mail?

I stripped charts from walls, emptied desk drawers,
heaved out a locked-tight metal box,
ran the chair at high speed on its wheels
against a glass-topped steel partition.

Then I paused and had second thoughts
about the mess I had inflicted
on my employers for their deceit.
Strangers gathered but kept their distance.

That moment I looked through the window,
same floor of the building next door,
saw a man in shirtsleeves whom I knew,
knew him well because I worked with him.

Likely they had called security
by now: nightsticks, uniforms, handcuffs.

I made for the elevators,
the office workers backed away —
this wrecker was not a bum, he was
a haywire image of themselves.

No one stopped me in the lobby.

I crossed to the block in which I worked,
the look-alike building to the south.

Do you have enemies? A question
they must have asked the occupant
when he returned from lunch. Owe loan sharks?

Sorry for the inconvenience caused.

I blame the glass-box architecture.

TAKEOVER

Shortly after California aeronautics flopped
Melvin, middle-aged, had to stoop to an editing job
and goad the company chess men in his first week at work.

I welcomed something new when I overheard his shrill
phone conversations with employee chess club members –
he told them he had watched them play and they weren't in his class.

I was bored out of my mind in the cubicle next to his
and I enjoyed the loud phone talk that burned up his working day.

Melvin took to calling various management levels
to pressure executives clutched high on the career ladder
to send him progress reports, which unquestioningly they did.

Some workers, half as old as Melvin, avoided him as weird –
everyone refused to sign the document he brought around.

The proclamation was grandiose, its wording notified
chairman, executive officers and board of directors
that herewith the employees had assumed company control.

Melvin entered a directors' meeting, announced the coup,
spelled out his terms for their continuing association
with the company under its employee leadership.

He held them chairbound for an hour, until one looked and found no
enraged employees slavering for blood outside the door.

No one hurt him. They escorted him from corporate quarters,
took security photographs, released him in the street,
told him not to come back, they'd forward his things and his pay.

That night Melvin broke a row of store windows somewhere in Queens.

BANK OF ELEVATORS

I press the down button, it lights beneath my finger.

The elevator doors slide open, it is empty.

Another pair of doors opens its metal petals
(something wrong with the computer?) and then another.

All three elevators wait, humming, clean, bright, empty.

Now the first doors move along their grooves, meet together,
then the second, the third, I hear sounds going away.

The light winks out within the elevator button.

HEAT, VISTAS, THE SOURCE, PACIFIC

A Mack truck, another load of frozen food,
        beating the red lights,
thunders by outside the window.

You cause my iron world reality
        to crash and burn,
throw me from the wreck I make of life

and keep me coming back for more
        of your sweet body.

ROOFTOP

Red legs and black toenails,
the pigeon struts and pouts,
hackles iridescent
pinks, greens, runs a circle
around his mate, bows, coos,
prepares to mount her back
to push against her in
wing-flapping ecstasy.

But she does not present
a submissive posture;
instead, walks off the roof
on a telephone line.

Despite virile ardor,
he finds this to be too
much a balancing act.

APRIL AGAIN

The first buds of maple reveal not leaves
but clusters of green flowers, green because
they have no need of color to compete,
so early in spring, with gaudy petals
for attention from pollen-coated bees.

A pigeon is dead on the fire escape
of the next building, beyond the maple,
belly down. Its mate hunches close to it
or brings in twigs, using its beak to push
them under the body to make a nest
for its eternally brooding partner.

Breeze ruffles the feathers and lifts a wing,
which doesn't scare a sparrow perched on top.
The small bird's beak plucks hackles for its home.

JONES BEACH, SEPTEMBER

Gulls stand on the uppermost reaches,
water flooding over webbed feet,
then ebbing over cheeks of sand.

The sun in murk a color spot,
a peculiar shade of red,
the beams are filtered by the smoke,
forest fires in Yellowstone park.

Carlos Santana plays guitar,
empty band shell, adjusting sound,
his concert starts at eight tonight.

Fathead jumbos circle offshore,
inbound delay at JFK.

Never seen the sea so calm before.

BUS STOP, JANUARY

Winter lights the bare-branched tree
coral-bleached in a warm sea.

Earmuffs, scarfs and thermal gear,
people wait, the bus stops here.

One shivers and others stamp,
they glance sideways at the vamp.

Her short skirt and her long legs,
she's not one of weather's dregs.

111 MOTT STREET

Chinese waiters, polite, smiling,
wait for the last eaters to leave.

Tsingtsao. Tsingtsao.

On a table, they place two chairs,
one upended on the other,
an ideogram: say farewell.

Tsingtsao. Tsingtsao.

BAG IN TREE

A white plastic bag
caught in a tree
(a gnarled sycamore's
witch-fingered twigs)
inflates and flaps
and sags, a wind-puffed
aerial condom

FRONTIER LIFE

I knew the color reproduction well
from books and magazines: a fur trader
dips a paddle in the smooth Missouri
from the stern of a dugout. Hides are piled
amid the craft. An Indian maiden
leans on them. Atop the prow, a black cat
with upright ears reflects in the water.

It always struck me as a touching show
of domesticity in wilderness,
Fur Traders Descending the Missouri,
George Caleb Bingham, 1845.

Exploring the real painting, I saw
two of my perceptions were mistaken:
the person leaning on the hides is not
a maiden but a young Indian man;
the cat silhouette contains a bear cub.

PHOTO OF 19TH CENTURY DIGNITARIES

This one terrorized his children.
And this one hardly knew their names.
Here is the one who might have been
poisoned by his wife. In God's name
this one liked to whip prostitutes
(he said: chastise fallen women).
Or was it this one? And this one
once dressed as Marie Antoinette.
The one with the sandy mustache
was the Czarina's first cousin.

NEW YORK CITY, 1904

The Flatiron building's northern edge
looms like the prow of a giant ship
out of an early blue-green photo.

This technological icebreaker
noses aside the lamppost gaslight's
wavery reflections on wet streets.

3

MIDTOWN ECOLOGY

A peregrine
        diving down the glass-walled offices

hunts pigeons
        fattened on corn kernels by old ladies

at park benches
        from plastic bags manufactured by

their offspring
        with no time to peer out office windows

SHE THINKS BACK

When McCarthy went on witch hunts
in the fifties, room dark, she saw
lantern slides of known communists
and she could not believe her eyes,
she raised her hand, stood up and said,
"Miss, that one's my Uncle Harry."
Kids shouted and threw books at her.

She recalled the shame days ago
on her mother's visit, who said,
"If you, as a young girl, were marked,
then think what things were like for me."
"For you?" She smiled. "A communist."

NEAR RHINEBECK

You'd think with all the trees they'd perch in them
           birds on a wire
unless they're urban birds unused to trees
           north for the day
on tour like us to view the autumn leaves

Artery-red corpse-yellow blotched with plague
           perched in the trees
a million faces peeping back at us
           souls of the damned
ready to tear loose when the next wind screams

PHOTOS FROM SPACE

The Hubble space telescope
beamed back photographs of them.

Eggshell blue and blossom pink
interstellar gas and dust.

Some of them appear to have
gargoyle heads and pointed ears.

And nothing more? Among them
shines a pointy Christmas star.

Its pulse signals from the void,
anchored to no Bethlehem.

UNSEEN PASSENGER

I shiver in the night air
and belligerent peer in
a taxicab back window
at a fussy man
who searches for his wallet
and selects a note
to pay his fare, who then counts
his change carefully,
calculates a tip
and puts away his money,
gathers all his packages,
looks around him to make sure
he's leaving nothing.

With apologetic smile
he holds the cab door open,
shuts it after me.

The taxi rolls on
slowly toward a red light.
I give my destination.
The driver steps on the brake.

A French name on his license.
From his head and neck, I see
he's black, skinny, fortyish.
Probably Haitian.

How did you get in my cab?
he asks. His voice is trembling.
He turns his head then
slow and peers at me
and his eyes, they look frightened.

I think he knows that
sometimes a zombie
wears a round, pink Irish face.

SIGNALS

The school for special children
opens its summer doors
to extra special children

down the block from where I live
and this July the playground
invisible to me

is auditorium
to adolescent male
continual distinctive whoops

repetitive as hiccups
mellifluously remote
off center

out of sync
with other children's voices
a hermit's song to earth

a lone voice on its lone journey
I heard a year ago
and hear again today

a vocal equivalent
of gamboling robot
electronic beeps

the whoops have urgency
yet sound reflexive
a method of location

calling to mind
the navigational honks
of geese on a star-filled night

a formation invisible
wingtip to wingtip
in migratory flight

NUDE

Her body lying back
damp with sweat
not hers, mine

and on her perfect breasts
some chest hairs
not hers, mine

      WAR CRY

    Today is a good day to die,
        the Lakota said,
meaning, I think, you had taken time out
        to confront, if not befriend,
the shades that linger in your spirit life
        and shake you awake
when you hide under the eagle wing of sleep.

    Do the grandmothers smile at you,
        the grandfathers nod,
    when you journey to places
        where the vanished rule?

CHRISTMAS ON THIRD AVENUE

You might have wanted, Christmas Day,
to twist and crack the air
in the avenue and cross streets
like ice cubes in a tray.

A couple outside a liquor store —
the security gate was down and locked —
bleary-eyed, disappointed, middle-aged,
she glared at him, he said to her,
Of course, I knew that it was Christmas.
What I didn't know, it was today.

TAPEWORM

After the Texas oilman B.L. Bourke
had expelled a whitish length of tapeworm
in a hospital suite the doctor said,
regardless of length, he would not be rid
of the parasite till they saw its head.

Next day, once more, B.L.'s bowels were purged
and yet another whitish length emerged,
again without the all-important head.

The doctor saw the gun beside the bed.

B.L. claimed he knew what he had to do:
Soon as this critter showed its goddam head,
put a slug between its eyes — kill it dead.

RAMADAN

I asked the taxi driver named Mahomet
if cool weather in New York had made it harder
to fast during Ramadan. He said, no,
it made it easier — it took your mind off
your emotions. In the Sudan, he remembered,
when the sun was directly overhead,
moving the bolts in the corrugated roof,
and you could drink no water yet for many hours,
that was where you knew God was talking to his people.

ARK

It starts innocuously ...
a spotted rabbit perhaps,
then cats of several kinds,
a turtle, a frog, a seal
and a crystal elephant.

It builds insidiously ...
ewes and lambs, a shepherdess,
collie dogs, a leprechaun,
a harp, a zebra, dolphins,
giraffe families, a goat.

Beasts continue to gather
and they stand in little herds
on sideboards of cherrywood,
windowsills, the mantelpiece,
tabletops and walnut shelves.

A ginger kitten, white bib
and feet, only three months old,
claws sliding on the polish,
breaks a few china creatures,
pieces the grandnieces hide.

MOURNING DOVE

The mourning dove
starts up his tune
before first light.

We hope he meets
a nice bird soon.

And when he does
we can expect
to hear him croon.

MESSAGE RECEIVED

Speaking of how people can be inclined
to take the things you say literally,
remember your friend who wanted a child
but could not conceive, even after she
had tried just about everything that she
could think of and then decided that she
should have herself checked out medically,
her husband also, and was found to be,
the pair, capable of procreation?

You explained about bicycling motion —
to think of her legs pushing on pedals —
to open her womb for seed to be sown
once her avid husband's climax was done.

She phoned to say you should get a medal —
your advice had worked beyond all belief,
she was three months gone, and what a relief
not to have to, anymore, leave warm sheets
and cycle madly up and down the streets.

A VISITOR BY NIGHT

a bumblebee
the size of a golf ball
droning like a World War II
superfortress but losing altitude when hit by tissue paper flak
hymenopteran dead reckoning
navigation
shot to shit
now
the dark

a light bulb

A WARM EVENING

Honeybees nuzzled the blossoms
    printed on her dress
and made her shriek and lift her hair.

At a wooden picnic table
    under maple leaves
she tongued the ice cubes in her drink.

An hour later I heard her laugh
    at something the men
had joked about who sat with her

before a row of clear plastic
    inverted glasses,
each with a loud imprisoned bee.

THIEF

I was a thief
and you had
power over me
and sent me to a place
where there was nothing to steal
and I stayed there
without stealing —
did that make me
more virtuous?

No, you deprived me
of moral choice —
I had no
opportunity to be
less virtuous.

A second question:
if you made me
no better,
did you make me
any worse?

Before you sent me away
I stole four times a week
but resisted
the temptation
eight times a week
and thereby exercised
some virtue.

By depriving me
of chances to steal
you stole from me
my virtue.

BOUQUET

On the arm of the groom
the bride in her white dress
came down from the altar
carrying white flowers.

You might have expected,
the woman said, roses
or some flower like that
but she embraced daisies.

Daisies would have been nice —
honest, simple and wild —
but as she came closer
I saw they were plastic.

THREE DIALOGUES

1
Ever kill anyone?

Two tours in Vietnam.

You killed people?

I killed people.

Do they ever come now
to you in dreams?

Yes, all the time.

What do they say?

I never know — they speak
Vietnamese.

That's a joke, right?

The joke's on me,
they tell me things
and I hear the lingo
but I never know
what they say to me.

2
You ever been
a crime victim?

I was hit on the head
with a hammer
by a serial killer.

Did they catch him?

No.

Did you know him?

No. He was a stranger
who saw me on the street
and hit me for no cause.

How do you know
he's a serial killer?

You can't go round
hitting women on the head
with a hammer
without killing some of them.

How do you know
he goes around
hitting women on the head
with a hammer?

Because that's what
he did to me.

3
Those roses are frozen.
When you bring them inside
their petals will open
and fall.

And how long will that take?

Four hours.

I'll have plenty of time.

LINDEN

The small linden tree
hardly ten feet tall
has overdone it

sprouting blossoms in
quantities greater
than look natural

like a teenage girl's
much too heavily
applied cosmetics

GRASS AND STUFF

It's frightening
in the suburbs:

all those kitchen windows
and behind each one
a poet looking out
philosophizing
about the backyard

WHO HAS WOKEN?

Who has woken
your sex kitten?

That dish you cooked
the other night.

The way you danced
on just one beer.

That look you looked
but wouldn't fight.

You feel aroused
but he's not here.

You're really hooked
and pull me near.

Someone's woken
your sex kitten.

TWITCH

Don't feel sorry for the girl
with neurological tics
opposite you
on the subway.

Beneath her hair, her earbuds
throb with music.

She is dancing.

OUT THERE

He had lived in the asylum
a long time exactly how long
he could not tell

He had newspapers and television
but somehow over time
he had lost touch

He had seen planes
orange flames of bursting bombs
people running and children

Television showed it happening
somewhere out there
where he might easily have been

Would he have curled up
in a cellar
with his thumb in his mouth

Or would he have jumped
from wall to wall
and danced among the flames

No one could predict
what he might do
out there in the real world

INTERRUPTED CALL

The man standing
talking on his cell phone
perhaps they thought he was speaking to them

the old pair
who had taken so long
to get off the bus and look around them

five feet tall
and both about ninety
the talking man never saw them coming.

The old man stood
close to the talking man
looked up and began to say things to him

while the woman
having caught her heel
in a grating had to clutch the arm

arm of the man
talking on the cell phone
who found it harder now to ignore them.

He pocketed
his little telephone
freed her heel and pointed their way to them

gazed after them
a moment bewildered
then smiled at a thought and reached for his phone.

A LANDMARK GONE

She discovered that her high school had been razed and in its place
squatted a multistory office block whose rows of windows
        glistened like scales.

I told her of a friend, daughter of a Kansas wheat farmer,
        whose family,
on sultry nights when the radio or television called
a tornado alert, slept in a cinderblock storm cellar
        beneath the house
and who emerged one sunny morning and found no house, only
        empty prairie.

She claimed she could accept the work of God or mother nature
        or whatever
more readily than greed of some property developer.

LAST WISH

Put my ashes in the river
that flows back and forth with the tide.

Up and down I'll wander
on Manhattan's East Side.

A SIGHT TO SEE

It takes a lot to draw a crowd
        to peer inside
        a store window
along Lexington Avenue.

Seven Abyssinian cats
        extend their necks
        and gaze as if
they lay along the ancient Nile.

Two blocks south I meet a painter
        and though I think
        his work abstract
I say to him they're worth a look.

He has no use for people who
        love animals
        and hate children,
he shouts and walks away from me.

It might help relieve his anger
        for him to spend
        a little time
curled up with cats in a basket.

HALLOWEEN

Don't assume in the West Village
that all the tall physically fit
women with brightly tinted hair
are drag queens. In this day and age
they could be tall physically fit
women with brightly tinted hair.

GET YOURSELF A DOG

The chihuahua stands fiercely on his toes
on the padded seat of an empty wheelchair,
      waiting anxiously.

Through its window, he tries to see inside the store.
Touch that chair and he'll tear you to pieces.
      Or thinks he will.

Gripping a cane in a malformed hand,
an elderly woman limps out of the store
      and calls to him.

Eyes popping, yipping nonstop, all four
legs stiffened, the little dog vibrates
      in excitement.

It brings to mind the sardonic advice:
if you want unconditional love —
      what you need to get.

ILL WIND

A shade flapped and pushed it from the sill,
it hit the carpet and didn't break,
and though I claimed it was hideous
and I'd hide it after you were gone,
I never did. Now an ill wind brings
the thought something has happened to you.

4

HOSPITAL FLOOR

Shrink the huge corridor
to Ancient Roman length,
its linoleum tiles
will become mosaic.

No Venus, Ganymede,
Neptune, goat or dolphin
cavorts across the beige
expanse this floor presents.

VIEW

You are the kind of person who notices
    the bluish silvery gray
        of river, buildings and sky
           or you are not

But do not underestimate people who
    need to have things pointed out
        before the perception strikes
           and we can see

INDEPENDENCE DAY ON THE HUDSON RIVER

The uppermost oak planks
of an abandoned pier
are bleached and weathered to
their spinal elements,
eaten by sun and wind
into brown dragon shapes.

We crowd the riverbank
to view tall-masted ships
parade the water in full sail.

This shore was clogged with sailing craft
when these top planks were newly nailed
upon the pier, the wind was fresh,
the sun was comatose
and horseless carriages were cheered.

ME AND THE MOB

After all this time
it's probably safe
now to confess.

I am the one
who sideswiped
the Cadillac

at 2 a.m.
outside the social club
on Mulberry Street.

It was double parked
and I sped away,
expecting bullets.

In time we learned
the FBI
had bugged the club —

they played the tapes
to nail the wiseguys
on conspiracy charges.

I want the court to know
that metal scrape you heard
was made by me.

WARNING GEESE

    Seven Canada geese
        twitch their heads and white chins
and rest their heavy bosoms

        on the Middle School lawn
        in the shade of a tree
in Westport, Connecticut,

        demonstrating perhaps
        in their anserine way
the risks of education

STYLE

Buy New York boutique socks
knitted by blind children
prisoners of Third World war

Socks organic in color
yellow for the desert
black for the jungle night
barefoot for evening wear

WOMAN WITH A QUESTION

She looked up and saw her mother
sitting in her window,
three flights above the ground.

She remembered what her mother
called, sitting in the window:
Why do you hardly ever
come to visit me,
you or your sister?

Next thing was, she saw her mother
push away from the window
and sail downward through the air

She must have closed her eyes.

She heard the sound of her mother
hit the ground beside her.

She looked in the blue eyes
of the handsome detective
who brought her a cup of tea.

Had it occurred to her,
he needed to know
though he didn't like to ask,
her mother tried to kill her?

She looked in those blue eyes
and saw cold laughter dancing there.

Had her mother tried to kill her?

She never told her sister.

Instead she discussed it
with men she met in bars
who listened attentively
to what she had to say.

She then asked their opinion.

Their eyes almost always
gave their thoughts away:

What kind of woman —
they were usually thinking —
would tell this kind of story
to some guy she had only
just met in a bar?

GOETHE HOUSE RECITAL

Mozart is known to have visited the house
while this clavichord was there, he said, wringing
his hands, so it's reasonable to assume,
I think, his immortal fingers touched those keys.

The furniture mover didn't seem to hear.
A large man in jeans, check shirt and biker boots,
he reassembled the early piano,
watched by anxiety clad in a gray suit.

My God, this instrument was imported whole
from Germany, he said. Yet, from Long Island,
you bring it here in pieces, a treasure not
taken apart in at least a hundred years.

The furniture mover was fetching a chair.
He sat at the keyboard, smiled and raised his hands.
He played. His nervous watcher kept his distance.
Ah, he said disapprovingly, Scarlatti.

ON THE SIDE OF A BUILDING

Uncovered, the painting on the bricks
is the height and width of the building,
not a scene with Venus or Bacchus —
after all, this is New York — a face,
a huge terra cotta colored face,
black eyebrows, black eyes and black mustache,
Mediterranean, Latino.

The paint on some bricks has paled or peeled,
creating a mosaic effect.
He must have meant something once to be
so big. Some archive may hold beliefs
associated with this image.
There they wait to be discovered
before his visage runs in rain or fades.

SPRING

Trees are shaking
their long antlers,
pawing the ground.

Their antler tips
tickle the clouds,
the clouds then drip.

This causes rain,
the trees must stop
that pawing sound.

THREE STORM WARNINGS

You know a storm is on its way when
the red-breasted sawbill diving ducks
arrive from bay and open water,
when winds draw stretch marks on river skin,
when the television weather folk
dance in front of radar weather maps

BANNER AND DRUMS

The Columcille Pipe and Drum Band
piped and drummed, piped and drummed its way,
Fifth Avenue, St. Patrick's Day.

The pipers headed for the pubs
when the march was finally done,
welcome anywhere, with a drone

and bag of air, leaving drummers
with their drums. In front of a bar
I met a drummer with his snare.

He knew I lived not far away
and asked if he and a few friends
who had marched and drummed in the band

could use my place to dump their things.
Seeing their instrumental plight,
I said I'd keep stuff overnight:

       a banner on two gilt-tipped poles
       of Columcille in Kingdom Come,
        five snares and the band's large bass drum.

He never phoned to pick them up.
Weeks went by, and my wife complained
space was lost, and her patience waned.

I phoned. The drummer was amazed,
said he couldn't thank me enough
and asked me where I found their stuff.

Band members were having meetings
to try to trace each man's movements
and try to pinpoint the moment,

unbelievable as it seemed,
when all their gear, treated with care,
just disappeared into thin air:

       a banner on two gilt-tipped poles
       of Columcille in Kingdom Come,
        five snares and the band's large bass drum.

TAXI ON LEXINGTON

When she was very young,
the taxi driver says,
her parents wouldn't let
her cut her hair. It grew
so long when combed it came
to the back of her thighs.

They stand out in traffic,
cars in tomato red,
not harsh — a soft red,
a tomato shade.

Her father said she
couldn't cut it till
she married and asked
her husband's permission.

The taxi is lemon.

Her kayak team had
planned a competition.
The water was cold
and if you tumbled in
with long hair and no
hair dryers back then
in Romania you
could get pneumonia.

They let her cut her hair.

GOOD MORNING

The cat jumped across the air shaft,
        five stories up,
to land upon a pigeon
on the opposite window ledge.

        It sank canines
through puffed iridescent feathers
        to seize the bird
        by its scrawny neck.

Holding the pigeon in its jaws,
        wings beating feebly,
the cat leaped back and entered
        the open window.

It placed its gift still throbbing
        beside the head
sleeping on the pillowcase
and waited for the clock to ring.

UNIDENTIFIED SAINT

I can guess the identity
of many saints from their statues
but I didn't know the bearded
gentleman in robe and sandals.

From the statue's placement and its
colorful plaster and large size,
he was a saint to reckon with.

A woman walked the church's length
to touch his foot and talk to him —
and left him with a playful slap.

ONLY A WAVELENGTH AWAY

      I don't have cable TV
and lousy highrises block my reception

      I was interested to see
a homeless guy in a wheelchair late at night

      on the sidewalk his TV
hooked to the base of a streetlight clear picture

      got me thinking it could be
the metal streetlight made a good antenna

WESTWARD

Snow covered the imperfections
of Union City, New Jersey.

Bill and I sat in the front, Bill
at the wheel, taking the highway.

The two women sat in the back,
involved in their realities.

Ann said, I've seen that spire before,
we must be going in circles.

Leave the driving to me, Bill said,
and we continued our talking.

Minutes later she said, That spire
again! We're going in circles!

I acknowledged that the two spires
had certain similarities –

might even belong to churches
of the same religious belief.

When the spire did not move it raised
another possibility.

I opened my door and said, Bill,
try keeping your foot on the gas.

The rear wheels spun in soft inches
of snow. Its untouched surface blurred

an exit lane. The car belly
rested on a traffic island.

Spires of old were travelers' guides
as this one was this snowy day.

ON THE WAY UP

When I saw my office looking south on midtown
on the twenty-eighth floor of the glass-walled highrise
I said to myself I must be more important
in my new job than I had anticipated
to be assigned such a clearly high-status view.

Being more important than I had expected
made me feel like a more responsible member
of society and almost a major cog
in the corporate gears though I a newcomer
was still learning to find my way to the men's room.

In May it was warm in June warmer in July
it suddenly dawned on me that only someone
wearing swimming trunks could remain behind my desk
in mid afternoon with the air conditioning
arranged for office comfort on the cool north face.

A FERRARI

My Buick
on blocks
outside

a rural cabin
would've been
an eyesore.

Take a ride,
its V8 engine
goes full bore.

No silencer,
foot to floor
hear this baby roar.

Leaving town
I pass a clown
in a Ferrari.

He stabs a finger
at his dashboard,
meaning radar.

I slow down
and see ahead
a police car.

Drive by
a Ferrari
and ask why.

ENLARGED DETAIL

After Wayne Alan Russo
the names of Edward Ryan,
John Joseph Ryan, Jr.,
Jonathan Stephan Ryan,
Matthew Lancelot Ryan,
Tatiana Ryjova,
Christina Sunga Ryook —

medical examiner's
list of dead and missing in
the World Trade Center attack —

Ryans, Ryjova, Ryook,
the people who did nothing
worse than go to work that day

FIRST ANNIVERSARY
OF TWIN TOWERS

The sixteen acre hole in the ground
could be mistaken for a building site —
no atmosphere of disaster
distinct from the everyday kind
to which we are all accustomed.

A ten minute walk from where I live,
the sidewalk is wide outside a firehouse.
Nine died from there: eight men, one woman.
The sidewalk is almost blocked by flowers,
ornamental plants and small bushes
in vases, bottles, earthen pots and
foil-covered plastic containers,
a daisy in a paper cup,
wreaths on stands, piled against the building.

Passersby have to walk around
this immense quantity of vegetation.
Most stop, stalled by the impact of emotion.

WHY ARE YOU WALKING?

What were you doing?
All you were doing
was walking daily
without waiting for
the photographers
to finish viewing
their loved ones posing
before a background
United Nations.

That is why you are
in many photos
in side view striding
on your daily way,
oblivious to
the photographers,
about to appear
in their viewfinders
as they clicked the shot.

In Japan alone
your image appears
in many thousands
of photographers'
shots of their loved ones
posing before the
United Nations.
This is not confined
to Japan alone.

It can only be
a matter of time
before an army
supercomputer
detects a pattern
in your recurring
image at this site.
The photographers
will not protect you.

SHOWER

There's no soap or no shampoo
among the bottles and tubes,
some of which stand on their heads,
with names like Apricot Scrub
or single-word labels in
elegant calligraphy
implying unreadably
that they may not be for you,
but no soap or no shampoo

LIVE PERFORMANCE

She searches endlessly in a bag.
        The bag is plastic.
        The acoustics
of Carnegie Hall amplify its rustle.

The orchestra is playing a slow movement.
        A smaller bag
           within the larger bag
may contain the thing for which she searches.

The smaller bag is also plastic
        and it rustles
           as she tussles
to locate still smaller bags within.

In time the rustling grows on me
        sitting near her,
           not hearing water
while dwelling next to a mountain stream.

QUANDARY

How does a poet persuade
people to read his poems?

As Joseph Schumpeter said,
it's not enough to produce
a satisfactory soap,
it's also necessary
to induce people to wash.

IT CAN'T BE HERE

I wake to a burning smell
in my fifth-floor apartment
and am already rationalizing
(it may just be boiler fumes)
already altering reality
before wakeful perception.

     As sirens approach
it's hard to remain under my blanket
     despite bitter cold
     till I can decide
by keen listening now fully alert
at which house exactly the sirens die.

They're not outside my building
I am fairly sure of that —
besides there's no commotion
in stairwell or corridors —
unless of course everyone
is lying still like me and listening.

     Shattering of glass
and the sound of a door ripped from its frame
(one of the kicks of being a fireman)
     someone calling to
     a victim perhaps
collecting the family photographs.

OBITUARY

After his death she told his life story,
beginning with infant wails of distress
being answered quickly by his mother,
which caused him to develop a secure
attachment to her, trusting in her
availability, showing a lack
of fearfulness, as such infants do.

She guessed this from his tranquil marriage,
since infants with secure attachments
go on to enjoy unconflicted
adult intimate relationships.

His father, when home, liked to take him
to look out to sea in heavy weather.

A DRIVE IN THE COUNTRY

Ken Kadish, Reuben's son,
in his furniture-moving days told me
he moved a woman's things
from Staten Island to south Ohio.

She asked him to move her
to some little town out in the middle
of nowhere, he did not
ask why and without maps did not know where.

He felt like a lonesome
solitary drive deep in the country
but when he saw her stuff
he said it would cost her less to throw it

away and buy new things
than truck it a third of the way across
America. She said
everything she owned was coming with her.

The woman could have been
his mother and Ken was none too pleased when
she climbed inside the truck
beside him and said she was set to go.

Across New Jersey and
Pennsylvania and then Ohio
it became a long haul
all day and all night into a new dawn.

Ken asked about the town —
Yellowbud, Elm Grove, Mount Joy or Good Hope,
I don't recall its name —
and she said that she had never been there.

She said she liked the name
and that was why she was coming to live
and though he might not see
things the way she did, she would need his help

in locating a house
to rent and from his point of view somewhere
he could unload his truck
and be rid of her and her paradise.

FRANCOIS

The doctor refused the quail eggs and champagne
at the trendy, monied art show opening.
He said, It's hard to believe that yesterday
afternoon I was treating starving children
in Ethiopia, and now I'm afraid
if I drink I might start yelling at people.

ASK NOT

The bell is saying its metal words
just loud enough to be heard
over evening traffic

Its heavy sounds drag themselves
along East 47th Street
to the United Nations

Gently slowly they resonate
in mature resignation
as daylight is fading

The tones hang in the air
outside a Japanese museum
in the middle of the block

I think of peace and order
and discipline and rice
and tranquility

But this bell peals next door
from a Catholic church
and it tolls for me

GREENWOOD MEN

Blow up a photo
to six feet in height
and ten feet across,

if the focus holds
almost anything
becomes an eyeful.

In full color on
a gallery wall
trees and undergrowth

stand in leaf on fields
in which wheat is shorn.
It may be France or

northern Germany,
the hills are gentle
and the sky is blue.

The trees and bushes
are nothing special,
hardly worth a look.

But stare at the leaves
till they undeceive.
Tell me what you see.

Men in camouflage
stand in open view
in front of the trees,

holding the matte stocks
of assault rifles,
and look back at you.

Once you have seen them
you can't believe how
you could have missed them.

Their faces are like
the stone faces high
on cathedral walls.

I HATE TO SAY IT

I don't know you and I
hate to say it but
your before and after
head shot photographs
in the newspaper ad
have got me thinking
you looked much better
with your previous face
than with the childish look
the surgeon gave you

ON 10th STREET

A big man who made very small sculptures,
George Spaventa kept tiny tropical finches
that darted in flocks around his windowless loft
lit by a domed skylight with side windows
operated by rope pulleys. They were open.
The birds could escape. If they want to go,
Spaventa said, they are free to leave any time
they wish. That's cruel, I claimed, you assume
they can decide for themselves what to do.
George looked surprised. That's what it's all about, he said.

THINKING OF HOME

With smiles the exiles think of home
in ways they never thought of home
when they lived in the land called home.

Think like we think, be more like us,
adopted homeland people say,
why would you want to be like you?

We do not want to be like us,
we are not who you think we are,
our children will not be like us.

Before we left we were like you
but here we changed to meet the things
regardless you expect from us.

We became what rumor declaimed
and saw familiar features
in history's specked looking glass.

Longtime exiles think of a home
in words they never found for home
when they grew in a place called home.

5

SUBWAY PASSENGER

I notice him enter the subway car
and stand by the door with outer borough
truculence and blood dripping from one sleeve
of leather jacket. He follows my look
down to the pool of blood starting to form
by his right foot, bright arterial blood
dripping in big drops, enlarging the pool.
He stares ahead. A stab or gunshot wound
maybe. I don't do a thing. If he keeps
losing blood he will hit the deck before
the train enters the tunnel to Brooklyn,
several minutes after I get off.

ON THEIR WAY

Today in New York City
the person who just shoved you
is less likely to be some
overenergetic male
from the inner city than
a financial services
employee with a college
degree in making money.

In a South Tower photo
after the second plane hit
but before the building fell
you can see people who are
not cops or firemen shoving
their way inside against the
stream of survivors-to-be
fast exiting the building.

NOT THIS RELIC

You are advised to cut in four
your driver's license once expired
to prevent its fraudulent use.

I sneer in some collector's eyes
scanning a horde of obsolete
licenses and certificates,

finding my face and wondering
what it was like to be alive
back then. I cut the thing in four.

ENCOUNTER

Two middle-aged
men staggered out
a saloon door
mid afternoon.

One scrutinized
a kid pushed
in a stroller
by his mother.

Get on your feet
and walk, he yelled.

The kid looked big
to be pushed
in a stroller
by his mother.

Get up and walk,
the drunk shouted.

His rage level
made his buddy
smile at mother
and shake his head.

CROSSING A STREET

As I walked against the light
and the car approaching slowed,
I gratefully waved and crossed.

He accelerated, braked,
called me a number of things
without saying why, drove off.

He perceived what came to mind,
instead of a grateful wave
he saw me give the finger.

HUDSON RIVER SOLITAIRE, NEAR RHINECLIFF

This Hudson winter evening
the sun drops without any
nonsensical visual display.

The river cold is blowing
as I walk alone along
the eastern bank's railroad embankment.

A ribbon of swamp is trapped
between the embankment and
what may once have been the river bank.

No trains running and no birds
flying and no fish jumping,
it is lonely in the fading light.

But this is what suits my mood,
this bleakness and cold and what
it must be like to have solitude.

Imagine my surprise when
men with guns stand up in blinds
and shout at me to get out of there.

LABEL

She handed me a bottle of wine
and said her husband would pick her up
sometime after midnight. I'd never
met her before – she was someone's friend
and seemed to know several people,
who greeted her. I gave her a drink.

She had brown eyes, full lips and big hips.
The wine she brought was Chateau Lafite
and I hid it where it would not be
poured accidentally. She said she'd
grabbed a bottle of her husband's wine
as she rushed out, late as usual.

A big man with wide shoulders and gold
teeth, a broken nose, he seemed annoyed
I said to take his wine with him when
they left. At a Manhattan party
nights ago his bottle of Lafite
had been dumped in the sangria bowl.

COMFORT SHOPPING

Three young women in a restaurant,
all having separately walked home
from Midtown to the East Eighties
on day two of the transit strike:
Did you buy anything? one asked.

How could I pass a thousand stores
and not buy something? one replied.

The third seemed relieved and told them,
I thought I was the only one.

NO SIXPACK

Are you off the brew?

The beer was never
for me – it was for
himself. He passed on.

Oh, he said, that's sad.

My bag is lighter
now he's gone, she said,
just reminding me.

Again he said, Sad.

It is, she agreed.

OUTSIDE A BUILDING

A white woman screamed.
A black man stood next
to her. We all looked
at him, as she kept
screaming. He pointed
to some bins. "A mouse,"
he said, nervously.

A DETAIL FROM REALITY

You can learn from TV shows like *Cops*
stuff you might easily overlook
or miss entirely in daily life,
for example, the tattooed guy who
called after shooting a tattooed friend
in what the guy claimed was self-defense.

Beside the body, on the tile floor,
lay a pizza slice, missing a bite –
found still clenched between the corpse's teeth.

Who would attack, an officer asked,
while biting on a slice of pizza?

WAITING TO CROSS THE STREET

A child in a stroller howled in rage
while her aggravated mother looked
another way and would not concede.

A young man in a business suit
looked at the child and urgently spoke
on his cell phone, perhaps explaining
to the beautiful woman he loved

that these were not the screams of a child
being slowly crushed by a truck's wheel
and that he was not standing aside
to avoid her blood on his new shoes.

JOKE AS POEM

You probably have heard this already:
the girl who is late for a concert asks
where Carnegie Hall is located and
nobody knows. She sees a man climbing
the subway steps with a violin case.
He will know. Please tell me, she asks, how do
I get to Carnegie Hall? Sadly he
whispers to her, Practice, practice, practice.

THE DARK SIDE

In his veins, egrets lift from the black
glistening mangrove roots. Iguanas
move their heads to look and caimans ease
beneath the liquid top, nostrils, eyes.

A disposable syringe dangles
by its needle from his upper arm.

He balances the wobbling canoe.

WHAT CAN WE DO?

Easy to say that she knows no other
kind of life, probably feels no deeper
pain as hope for change recedes with greater
age, she never could be called a weeper,
always proves herself to be a keeper
of commitments, concedes that she can err,
oh what in the world can we do for her?

SUBWAY FOAM

You can come home from work and get
major sleep and then head out
for activities prolonged
into the early hours
of the following day
and show up for work on time.

This was what he was doing when
he overdid the alcohol
and during a stop at home
to quench his continuing thirst
he ate a couple of quarts
of strawberry ice cream.

On the subway to work he
had a gastric attack
in a crowded passenger car
and blew pink bubbles from his mouth
like a diver under water
releasing bursts of oxygen.

He remembered how people
emptied the car around him
as he regurgitated streams
of pearlescent popping bubbles
a powerful memory
the nausea of strawberry.

CAWK SPOKE SQUAWK

Two Asian women talking very loudly
on the bus were interrupted by a male
Cawk who spoke their language. Seemingly upset,
they soon got off. What were you saying to them?
his wife asked. I never heard anyone here
speak Squawk before — it's not what I said, he said,
but the fact that someone here could understand
what they were saying. I might have made them lose
their sense of privacy in America.

A GOD OFFENDED

Out of nowhere lightning strikes
a late-model family car
on Lexington Avenue
going slow in the center lane.

An eccentric javelin
of flame hits the car's steel roof
and jumps a moment later
to a steel manhole cover
the car has just passed over,
hitting with a loud report.

The car stops, its hazard lights
are blinking, its driver
emerges cautiously,
waves traffic by in other lanes
and looks at the wheels and paintwork,
puzzled and unaware of this
bolt from the quiver of Zeus,
sky god, lord of the wind, clouds, rain
and thunder, omnipresent,
omniscient and omnipotent.

You can smell ozone in the air.

STAR TREK ENCOUNTER

First my daughter and then my son,
seven and nine at the time,
in the park near the mayor's
official residence,
stopped and stared at a man.

At the iron rail
high above the draining tide
stood the first officer
of the starship *Enterprise*.

Without a trace of a smile
Spock looked at my children,
held up his right hand
in the Vulcan salute and said,
Live long and prosper.

This was years ago and even then
Leonard Nimoy must have had enough
of Mr. Spock, yet he behaved
with dignity

as a representative
of the planet Vulcan
and with the decorum expected
of a Starfleet officer.

We walked some way before
my children managed a word.

WEAVING CAR

The car ahead is weaving
over the nearly empty
eastbound concrete expanse of

the Cross-County Expressway.
Giving the car a wide berth
I accelerate past and

watch in the rearview mirror.
The car creeps up to pass me
and I let it go because

I'm driving with my children.
As the car passes I see
it is packed with teenage guys.

Ahead once more the car slows
and moves to block me and then
moves aside to let me pass.

Out a back window a guy
aims a revolver but sees
my kids next to me and hauls

the snubnose gun back inside.
I know he has a mother
who some day in tears may tell

the media reporters
that to her he was always
a good boy and loving son.

SINGING WOMAN

She has an awful voice she says
and after only a few sips
of alcohol she gets an urge
to sing and then she cannot stop.

Her friends all say don't offer her
a drink or you will see that she
can drive you crazy and us too
although we like to hear her talk.

6

HOUR OF DEPARTURE

Some say they favor the hit-or-miss
style of Arthur Rubinstein over
the manicured manipulations
of the great Vladimir Horowitz,

not on my mind as I walked in the
Nineties between Park and Lexington
in the very early morning hours
when people asked me to be quiet

since Mr. Horowitz was dying –
gentle vigilantes who appealed
to all that was kind and good in me
to let the great man expire in peace.

It seemed then a misunderstanding
that he might prefer to shuffle off
his mortal coil in total silence
than hear distant singing in the street.

CONSTRUCTION SUPERVISORS

Two supervisors talk
at a construction site,
clad identically in
hard hats, jeans, gloves, work boots
and luminescent green
safety vests. One jumps
up and down to keep warm.

Through my binoculars
I ascertain the fact
without further doubt this
is indeed a woman.
A man would never jump
up and down to keep warm.

INWARD EYE

A psychiatrist told me women thought
he could look into their innermost depths
when he knew with little more than a glance
how their lives had gone since he saw them last.

All he did was look at her hair and knew
when a woman felt good about herself.

CONJUROR

Flash the six of hearts and seven of diamonds
and quickly place these two cards face down on top

of the pack you placed face down on the table.
Use power of mind to cause these two cards to

migrate downward by magic to the bottom
of the pack. Then pick up the pack of cards and

flash the six of diamonds and seven of hearts
previously placed by you on the bottom.

Shuffle the cards and do not repeat the trick
and note how many believe and few observe.

MIGRATING BUTTERFLY

A monarch butterfly flapped inside
the glass door of Commerce Bank. He held
the door open so that it escaped
outside and resumed its journey south.

A woman just then exiting the bank
was touched by his humanity and smiled
at him. He said a lot of butterflies
visit this New York bank on their journey
south and visit next the Miami branch.

Alarm flickered in her eyes, alarm
on letting down her guard a moment
with an unknown man and seeing him
change from touchingly kind to plain weird
in a moment, over butterflies.

SUPERMARKET INCIDENT

Their green skulls freshened by time-controlled mist,
boston, romaine and iceberg smile at me
in rows. I select a head and I shake
water from its drenched leaves. A woman screams.

MEMORIAL AT FIRST AND 49TH

A ghost bicycle sprayed white is chained
to a street lamp in memoriam.
Cardboard tells her name but only says
hit by a car not whether it was
a hit and run. I think of her not
as one of those heavy brutes who ride
helmeted and knee padded and who
speed with homicidal negligence
among the elderly and infants
unprotected and unexpecting.
I think she wobbled in a long skirt
and was laughing on her telephone.

PATIENT BREAK

The old guy already had two thirds
of his body inside the saloon,
clutching the door protectively to
his chest as he talked to a woman
outside, much younger, a caregiver.
You can't come in – you would lose your job,
he said, take a walk around the block.
It's raining, she said. I won't be long,
he promised. She muttered unamused
in her language things known about men.

COUPLES

1
You look like one of those,
he said, pink wild roses.

She sniffled and replied,
I feel more like ragweed.

2
Looking in a diamond dealer's window,
we see a hundred chips of what might be
very expensive disappointing glass.

When we turn to go, an angle of light
hits with the optics of a welder's torch.

3
She asked, Did you see her shoes?

He asked, Did I see her shoes?

I saw you looking at her –
surely you noticed her shoes.

I didn't look at her shoes.

4
I think
I'll make
carrot soup,
she said.

Where will you
find them?
he asked.

Find what?

The parrots.

5
Please don't make me laugh,
she said. I feel like
staying mad at you.

6
Just when she
got all her
movie posters hung
the way she wanted
them he

7
He danced the dance move, and she said,
You look like one of those people
cast in ash by Vesuvius

TELEPHONES

1
A woman chatting on her telephone
while standing in a supermarket aisle
holding row upon row of cans of beans
unthinkingly reaches to rearrange
some of them so their labels now face out

2
I'll say no more about women
talking on mobile telephones
now I've seen a man with a phone
stand at a urinal and piss
and not miss a word of his call

A LESSON IN PRICING

It was all for charity so
he set a price of five dollars
for every book on the table
but did not sell one in two hours.

The director of marketing
thought it a hoot he was a goof:
she upped the prices, then slashed them,
most from thirty dollars to ten.

He sold nearly all of the books
within an hour despite the fact
they were now double the price
of what they had been before.

GENERATIONS

She, her daughter grown,
chats while grandson roams
in grandmother's home.

This feels good, he says.
His small hand squeezes
a breast prosthesis.

Grandma says in fun,
This shows his tastes run
in our direction.

IN A CROSSTOWN BUS

"I don't want to speak to you – let me speak to Josephine,"
                            she says on her telephone.
                Someone behind loudly masticates
                            crackly junk food.
                The bus waits as a truck blocks the lane.

"If I wanted to speak to you, I would have asked for you –
                        let me speak to Josephine."
                Someone behind is tearing a new
                            crinkly package.
                The driver stops for wheelchair access.

"I said I won't speak to you – let me speak to Josephine."

IN BROOKLYN

An old guy walks the local market aisles,
consulting a list and choosing items.

Other old guys play golf or walk the beach –
he likes to shop for food his wife will cook.

Two thugs shadow him. They keep their distance
and keep an eye on him and on the door.

Finished, he wheels his cart to the cashier,
a young guy who's all mouth and attitude.

This guy likes to show he does not respect
the old guy with his list and shopping cart.

The thugs know the look on the old guy's face
when he means that they should keep out of things.

Eventually the young guy hears about
who it is he has been disrespecting.

My God, he thinks, the Godfather did not
have them break my legs, and now he is quick

to greet the old guy with the cart and say,
Yes, sir, no problem, Mr. Gambino.

One day the old guy looks at him and says,
You were better the way you were before.

BY THE WAYSIDE

I stepped over them every sunny afternoon
        as they rested weary selves
                on warm concrete.

Where are they now? Gone, like the snows of yesteryear.
        The city fathers found them
                resting places

        I know not where –
but where supine forms would not diminish the price
        of property per square foot.

        Yes, back in the days when they
lay like fallen leaves in unseasonal descent
        on city streets

a visiting friend from early years was appalled
        by the callous way in which
                I stepped over

        fellowmen abandoned to
alcohol or drugs or diabetic coma
        and decided

his heart had not hardened to the needs of others.
        He would not pass
another soul in despair.

        The next one lay on his back
                in peaceful sleep.
He shook him awake and asked if he needed help.

The man tried feeble punches and called me by name
        to give him help
against the guy shaking him.

        I asked him when he had stopped
                taking his meds
and how many pints of vodka a day he drank.

        For the misunderstanding
my friend donated twenty dollars, an amount
                not disputed.

ADVICE TO THE POLICE ACADEMY

      I felt I would be attacked
by two loitering malcontents who looked somewhat
            tougher than me.

      With no escape,
I made no attempt to sidestep what seemed my fate
         and looked them cold in the face.

      Lawmen's predatory eyes
          returned my gaze
and neither made a move as I walked slowly by.

Street attackers nearly always avoid your stare
         and look sidelong
     at this or that, up or down.

      These two plainclothes officers
         had yet to learn
role players can't afford to have judgmental eyes.

      Women know it very well:
they estimate a man's potential at a glance
         and look away.

PEDESTRIAN CROSSING

A car turned the street corner
        fast and hit
        the bag

of library books I held
        to protect
        my gut.

The books thumped against a door.
        Hit and run,
        no way,

the car stopped. The driver stepped
        out to look
        at me.

I guessed that he might be on
        probation
        and so

he could not take the risk some
        minor thing
        like a

highway code infraction might
        put him back
        inside.

I yelled obscenities and
        shook my fist
        at him.

He seemed much relieved to see
        with his own
        two eyes

that the fool he hit could still
        dance and sing
        in rage.

KNOCK ON THIS DOOR

every hour
until someone
tells you something.

Do not do
what this person
tells you to do

because this
may be
psychosis.

NOVEMBER

The wind has stripped the leaves from their tops
        and now the November trees
display any leaves still intact and
        youthfully jump in the wind
        like men prematurely bald

&

        The two poodle-shaped dogs have
        a light golden fur almost
invisible in the golden leaves
as they bury their noses and run,
        creating parallel wakes

SWEET ASSASSIN

Passport photos in rows
on a newspaper page
in color, eleven
men and four women, some
better in appearance
than others, two or three

might even have problems
with personality,
faces average you
could say for almost
any group except for one
face that jumps out at me.

Her eyes are large and brown,
her lips are sensual
and have a humorous
upturned personal twist
that suggests intimate
contact and whispering.

These passport photographs
show foreign visitors
that intelligence claims
are hit team members who
smothered an arms buyer
with his hotel pillow.

I think she needs to hide
and now I have her here
beside me naked on
my bed and doing things
that I will not inflict
on you, my listener.

We rest a moment, skin
to skin, and this is when
she turns confessional
and whispers in my ear:
Darling, there is something
you should know about me.

SORTING MAIL

I noticed a man in a dark suit
climb the entrance steps in front of his
private home on a Manhattan street,
unlock the outer glass-paneled door,
unlock the mailbox, turn around and
come outside with a handful of mail.

He raised the lid of the garbage can
and placed it to one side, examined
each envelope as if its contents
were seeping through and discarded most
unopened as if denying home
entry to undesirable fish.

Although I don't own a home, I thought
a method like this could work for me –
were it not for the fact that I know
I would have to return to the can
in less than twenty minutes or so
to search for needed pieces of mail.

RESPONSE

Your eyes do not work
like a camera.

Your brain constructs its
images with what
you already think.

A quarter of all
brain activity
is involved in this.

You think these poems
are like photographs.

7

A NEW MYTHOLOGY

Someone said that Victorian women
did not have the education required
to stuff their poems with mythology
and thus are often readable today.

It's great not to have to look at notes on
Phaedra's relations with Hippolytus
but I notice a sprinkling of new names
in things I read. These people seem not to

do the abominable things with which
the Ancient Greeks sometimes amused themselves.
The Greeks never had to go to rehab,
never performed community service.

LIKE IT IS

He was surprised, a public relations man,
to be asked to speak at the graduation.

He put together what he thought was needed
for graduating Americans to hear.

You think God may want them to die for Wall Street –
they will not accept that, a colleague remarked.

He tried a rewrite but it said the same thing.
On a very early train north to the school

he had no ideas. He sighed and picked up
the New York Times. Six stories on the front page.

He recognized who had placed four of the six.
Here was his speech! These kids don't know what's out there.

Do they think reporters fan like honeybees
from the busy Times hive in search of stories?

And whose thoughts can they expect to influence?

Men who beat pizza dough and know what they know
or readers proud of their independent minds?

UNDERGROUND

Beneath the twigs and bitten grass
the blue and yellow rioters
pushed and hosed are struggling upright
in knowledge that their time is come
and that they cannot now be stopped

the crocuses are shouldering
the winter soil restraining them

SURPRISED BY GULLS

She took crusts of bread to feed the sparrows
on foot-thick snow beside the East River.

The ring-billed gulls wheeled around, clamoring,
wingtips at times almost touching her face.

I saw two young men ahead, without coats
at freezing point, lean on the rail and look

out over the water – to me it seemed
an unlikely pause to admire the view.

They waited for us to pass beyond them
to where the path through snow had no escape.

When I called to her the excited screams
of gulls around her head drowned out my voice.

She threw crusts in the air quite near the men
and the gulls mobbed them with frantic circling,

backing them away. She returned to me,
bread exhausted, and we retraced our steps.

Again they looked out over the water,
again resumed their predatory wait.

THROWING OUT A BOOKCASE

A lightweight ramshackle bookcase
being carried by two women,

all legs and arms, bare and shapely,
out the door of an apartment

on the ground floor blocked my entry
and I volunteered assistance

to discard it on the sidewalk
and joked with them on their reading.

They were busted six weeks later
with whips, handcuffs and rubber stuff

and with the man who often sat
alone in a car parked in front.

I heard he ran the show inside
without setting foot in the place.

And now what about the bookcase?
Look at it from their point of view:

what could they do with a bookcase?
No one is as kinky as that.

LATE AFTERNOON, FIRST AND 88^(TH)

She walked her walk in high-heeled boots with dangling pom-poms,
a grown woman, much beyond the youth, probably high,
who stooped behind her and tried to catch the bobbing playthings
as she strode beyond his reach without a backward glance.

He straightened up and turned for approval to his friends,
five of them, their schoolbags on the ground, who had held back,
all of them near six feet tall and almost two hundred pounds,
none showing a wish to rob, molest or interfere.

If he had knocked the woman to the ground the charge could be
assault and while she and he were white, his friends were black
and although this was Manhattan not Alabama
nonparticipation might not be enough in court.

As I approached, I thought up friendly words to warn them of
the legal risk of such nonprofit activity
and noticed them step backward and look another way,
clearing the stage for a thing about to happen here.

Had he surprised me, my white assailant would have downed me –
I moved with him and tried to bang his skull against a car
and though he broke away I was satisfied to have
communicated in language I think they understood.

LIMOUSINE DRIVERS

    Limo drivers
park waterside and eat
    their lunches

    Plastic-boxed
Central European
    food items

    One feeds gulls
on his weight-loss diet
    just perhaps

    Gulls pester
in his absence other
    limo drivers

    To the gulls
all the limo drivers
    seem alike

ART COLLECTION

A painter tells me he will very soon be forced
    to throw out his unsold canvases
    accumulated over the years
    because they occupy working space.

He foresees a public television program
    about a sanitation worker
    accumulating over the years
    a thrown out canvases collection

that he plans to donate to an art museum
    in a building to be named for him.

GIRL IN ART MUSEUM

In these museum portraits, I suppose
I hardly notice the foreground figures,
the ones the artists were paid to compose,
and look instead at background trees in rows,
lakes, guitars, archangels, dogs in corners,
a girl in the Metropolitan says.
He was a king and *she* was an empress?
They look like people on a city bus,
the kind you hope won't sneeze on you or, worse,
contrive to rub their bodies against yours.

STREET ART

Twelve hundred years ago Yuan Chen
      told his friend the poet
Po Chu-i that he had seen a poem
brushed by him on the outside wall of an inn

and had to use his expensive coat
      to wipe away the moss
hiding some calligraphic characters
in order to read the complete thing.

No one previously bothered to do so,
      Po Chu-i responded,
hypersensitive in that way in which
poets react to well meant comments.

Imagine rival poets back then
      defacing poems, and
every now and then offended authorities
must have ordered walls to be painted clean.

Does moss gather on street art today?

APRIL IS HERE

The buds are budding,
the daffodils are popping

and I imagine an earthy smell
in the springtime city air

in which there is a little chill
but one that does not interfere

with women in a backyard laughing
who sound as if they have been sipping

HOSPITAL TOMATOES

Each morning doctors arrived with tomatoes handpicked behind their suburban
                homes
and looked for city-dwelling colleagues to appreciate taste ripened on the vine.

I carried four bags home and had to look for other city dwellers to eat them.

As days passed and we tired of the joys of all at one time ripening tomatoes
if we could we avoided medical doctors approaching us with bags in hand.

A doctor insisted I accept a bag of what he called "rescued" tomatoes
telling me how an hour ago while he stood on his hometown train station
                platform
he lifted the lid of a garbage receptacle in order to dump his wife's
slowly picked garden gifts only to see it already half filled with tomatoes
and had not the heart to abandon his own bagful of what he called family
survivors that he now trustingly was handing over to my personal care.

CHANGED TIMES

They talked of glimpses still to be had of old New York
and I pictured Lincolnesque men and graceful women
       who lifted petticoats over curbs
but they referred to street scenes of the 1960s
       and how they now had almost vanished.

       No doubt you've heard the streets of Paris
were quelled by television and better home plumbing
       and by higher prices in cafes.

Once I believed that people enjoyed life in the streets
       more than captivity in small rooms.

Some might have dreamed with the poet in China who dreamed
       of a thatched hut on a mountainside.

TRY LOURDES

A godless psychiatrist often encouraged
patients to visit Lourdes. A miraculous cure
       is what you pray for.

He believed many physical maladies are
secondary symptoms of an underlying
       depressive disorder.

If you can alleviate your depression
your physical symptoms can as if by miracle
       suddenly disappear.

In Lourdes you see the desperate exaltation
of the spiritually aroused, beyond hope
       of a physical cure

through conventional medicine, and their aura
has an oxyacetylene glare that destroys
       the fabric of despair.

You are moving across the stones upon your knees.

NEIGHBOR

          You've seen a brain-damaged man
take occupancy of a place on a street
      where no one demands his removal

      He has his own possessions
which he arranges around himself
and things kind-hearted people give him to eat

You hardly notice him anymore
      seeing him there every day
always in the same place and at the same time

      Until one day you notice
now the sidewalk is clean and empty
and you never see or hear of him again

YOGA

    Standing on one foot
while I pull a sock on the other foot –
about as far as I care to go with
      yoga positions.

A friend claims yoga has kept him limber
      and as he explains
      I think of the time
his son entered the gym and saw someone
      with heel behind neck
surrounded by the members of his group
      female and concerned

saw that the person locked in position
      was his own father
and decided that now was not the time
      to come to his aid.

UNTITLED

He warned me not to step
on any roaches and
to brush them off the chair
before I sat. This was
meant for their sake, not mine.

He never mentioned mice
running all over me,
looking for things to eat
but in a friendly way.

My food stayed unopened:
sliced Virginia ham,
sliced American cheese
and a loaf of sliced bread.

A visit days later:
ham and cheese on the floor,
mice and roaches at work,
mold consuming the bread,

the mice ignoring me
the way golf course rabbits
ignore people with clubs
savagely swiping at
the balls in the grass that
they consume placidly.

THIEVES

Still chained, a bicycle frame
picked clean as a chicken bone.

Thieves contribute to our lives
by keeping them lean and mean.

When they broke into my place,
rooted around and then left

without taking anything,
why did I feel insulted?

DAYBREAK

Before she left I sat up in bed
and promised her I would do that day
a number of things she needed done.

I do not remember this event.

When I said yes to her verbal list
she should have known immediately
that one of us had to be dreaming.

HOLIDAY PIZZA

The man behind the counter
serves me a slice of pizza.

I ask, What are they doing
with the wire and the ladders?

They're putting up Christmas lights.

But isn't this place Jewish?

This is a pizzeria.
My people come from Naples.

I worry about my slice:
You mean this isn't kosher?

A man behind the counter
laughs and speaks Italian. The

one who looks like he wants to
kill me then takes my money.

BEFORE DAWN

Before dawn I swig antacid
and look out a window
at people running.

Those raised in the years
of governmental plenty
with benefits galore

to usher them comfortably
out of this world
behave like there's no tomorrow.

Now that hope of benefits
is going or gone
why run in predawn street light

punishing body to extend
life into almost
certain deprivation?

EAST RIVER VIEWS

1
The East River, its turgid
oiled discolored tidal bulk
running against whatnot, deep,
lit by dawn and blown by wind,
ruffles and calms and reflects
thoughts rippling across its brain,
perhaps

2
A pale hand of fog
lifts off the water
and runs its fingers
between the buildings,
careful not to break
those tall and fragile

3
An October afternoon,
among debris outgoing
with the tide, down the river,
beneath the glass-skinned buildings,
a brown goose, head under wing

4
A cheddar moon
in the raspberry haze
low over Brooklyn
other side of the river

5
The plates of ice on the black water
palpitate in the wake of barges.
They slide with the tide and crowd in herds
along the bank, nudge against the dock
and collide – with a fragile tinkling.

6
Riverside lights
on black water
make yellow bars
smeared by movement

7
      A pod of kayaks
invades the navigation path of
    a barge pushed upstream
          almost submerged with
its load of liquid hydrocarbons
    and another barge
        being towed downstream
its bulk completely out of water
    weightless emptiness

8
The green light to port
and red to starboard,
the barge is coming
directly at you

8

VOLUNTEER

I offered to wash the dishes. I claimed
I had professional experience
in this field, although none recently,
      I was happy to say.

Some implements that I took in hand
bewildered me, and I turned them around
like a future archeologist
      pondering their use.

Do archeologists of the present day,
in the dustfree quietness of long rooms,
ask the people who mop the floors
      or chop vegetables

if they recognize any ancient tools?
Might it have been used to polish oak?
      Or core apples?

NEW YEAR AWAKENING

It was snowing as I waited in line
outside Trader Joe's liquor store
and joked with a woman behind me:
"You know you have a drinking problem
when you stand in line in weather like this."

What I said touched a nerve. She left without
a word – I never got to say I was
only joking. I think of her
as dry and happy, as someone who can
weary friends by redescribing
the incident that changed her life.

RADIO TIMER ACCIDENTALLY SET

It was music of a serious kind
and I wondered about the band outside
at nearly six thirty in the morning –
I could see a clock where I lay in bed –
I could hear the music was not moving,
it did not seem to be a marching band
and sounded anyway more symphonic,
not coming from the street as I had thought,
the fifty instrumentalists or so
must be crammed into many tiny yards
behind the houses and I drifted off
considering the logistics of this

IN PASSING

1
Tracey Emin,
the painter, says
that she judged love
by what she got
but now she thinks
she should have judged
by what she gave

2
The Goncourts noticed that nothing is repeated:
not the physical pleasure a woman gave you
one particular time, not an exquisite dish
you ate. You'll never have exactly that again.

3
     As John Berryman
leaped to his death from the upper deck
of the Washington Avenue Bridge
over the Mississippi River
     the lone onlooker
saw that John Berryman waved at him

OUT OF TOUCH

Starved Bolshevik rebels
invaded the palace
of a Russian princess.

They said they'd spare her life
if she showed them the way
to the palace kitchen.

She said she had never
been there and so had no
idea where it was.

George H.W. Bush,
seeking reelection,
tried a supermarket.

The barcoded checkout
amazed him, which told some
he had not bought his food

or household things for years.
The princess was intrigued
by cooks preparing food.

The Bolsheviks eating
were amused: she ended
safely in Switzerland.

The media people
did not smile: Mr. Bush
had to leave the White House.

STRANGE PEOPLE IN SUBWAYS

If you get a seat in a crowded subway car
      close your eyes.
You soon hear a dominant voice, often someone
      standing near
you, a man or woman you cannot see because
      of closed eyes.
Do not open them. Instead, listen to that voice
and visualize the person it belongs to.
      Sometimes I
alarm people when I stare at them amazed at
how they differ from the people I listened to.

AARP: 99 GREAT WAYS TO SAVE!

Plastic shower caps make wonderful food
storage covers, and baby socks, stretchy
and colorful, make cheap cellphone covers.

The American Association
of Retired Persons made these suggestions.
I hear a near family member say:

The first we knew something might be wrong was
when she put plastic shower caps on food
and a little sock on her telephone.

STAR PERFORMER

I worry about
a fearsome nun
in Paradise
sidling up to me
like an Olympic
woman boxer
and saying to me:

I hope it was worth
all those coins you
inserted to light
my corpse in the box
where they put me
in the dry crypt
of that cathedral.

HEADLINE

Eighty six year old woman
falls off cliff while raking leaves.

Ponder a headline like that,
who needs to read the story?

Folk want a happy ending:
caught in a tree branch halfway
down, she was rescued unharmed.

And the leaves? They whirled into
a little heap of compost
on which wild strawberries grow.

SUSPICION

She was seeing someone,
he said, he did not know
who but knew when because
she always washed her hair.

Jealously paranoid
was what she would call him
if he confronted her,
a diagnosis that

might possibly hold up
unless he spied on her
and caught her in the act,
a thing he would not do.

Americas

1

CHRISTMAS

Helicopters
drop hay to deer
on the mountain.
The snow is fat.

FROM WEBSTER'S THIRD
NEW INTERNATIONAL DICTIONARY

hollyhock: a deep purplish red
that is bluer and deeper than Harvard crimson (sense 2)
or American beauty
and redder and duller than magenta (sense 2a).

magenta (sense 2a): a deep purplish red
that is bluer and stronger than American beauty,
bluer, lighter, and stronger than hollyhock,
and bluer and deeper than Harvard crimson (sense 2).

Harvard crimson (sense 2): a deep purplish red
that is redder and paler than hollyhock
or magenta (sense 2a)
and stronger and slightly bluer and lighter than American beauty.

American beauty: a deep purplish red
that is redder and paler than hollyhock,
redder and less strong than magenta (sense 2a),
and less strong and slightly redder and darker than Harvard crimson (sense 2).

PUSH
LLUP

blue sky

t   e   h
h   n   e
i   d   r
s   s   e

another case of that

           grass

the
    semidomesticated
                  slow
                        death
                            of
                               the
                                  stricken
                                      dove

ASTRONAUT IN THE AFTERNOON

Heaven is blue eternity

    around the globe
    above the winds
that drag the clouds in patterns good for weather forecasting
in a cumulonimbus greenhouse atmosphere.

    No vertigo,
    floating

    too high up
to tumble down screaming and waving your arms
in the air-writing reflex of an animal falling.

    Sun shines by
    without heat
and the aluminum-honeycomb petals of the solar power machine
    open without a sound.

    Tonight for dinner
    algae,
which renew the oxygen and live on sunlight and expired breath
    in purified urine.

    Out here,
    to turn a screwdriver
    would send you flying.

    With feet
planted firmly on the ground,
argument exists.

Maybe it's lack of gravity's force on the inner ear ...

Lack of everyday sights, sounds and smells ...

    I gaze
at a planet in hope
my rooftop will come into view.

LEAVES

        Louis grows
    becomes aware
of how the seasons move

        how the leaves
    green on the trees
when the weather grows warm

        fall to ground
    before Christmas
when the weather grows cold

        again are
    back on the trees
when the weather grows warm.

He asks, How do the leaves
get back up on the trees?

SILENT WOOD

Silent
wood evergreen
hardwood summergreen
deciduous comb-claw
beetle radiosensitive
tree comb-footed
spider fern
frond

deep in the silence of the wood
stand still

hear
forest noises

REAL-WORLD SCENE

   A Roman poet
on a visit to Nevada,
      foreseeing
   the doom of civilization
on the future light cone of space-time,
      soundlessly
as the ultrasonic postejaculatory song of the male rat
     folds his tent
and moves away across colossal ruins
    of wind-blown desert sand

THE WITCH AND DAFFODIL

Once ago
in the trees
an old witch
with gray hair
fed pigeons
yellow corn.

The old witch
was covered
with black rags,
the pigeons
thought she was
a tree trunk.

She scooped more
yellow corn
from a brown
paper bag
deep in her
shopping cart.

The pigeons
flapped, circled,
perched upon
her shoulders,
pecked and shoved
at her feet.

The old witch
gazed fondly
on her birds,
little ones,
featherbrains,
gobbling corn.

Along came
Daffodil,
her daddy
taking her
out walking
in the park.

Daffodil's
combed and brushed
curly hair
wasn't gray
and her clothes
weren't rags.

The old witch
saw her and
bared her teeth,
what some might
call a smile,
some, a snarl.

The small girl
danced on the
yellow corn,
the pigeons
panicked, flew
in the air.

Daffodil
laughed, the witch
moaned spells on
one who'd made
her pigeons
fly away.

FIVE MINIATURES

1
snow hare
where?
there!
nowhere
no hare

2
Do the leaves
hang sullen
on the trees?

3
A valentine:

onto a heart
attach six legs
and a pair of
long antennae

4
Out in the black
ether of space
the stars lie hit
like tennis balls

5
You hover at the flower
and drink nectar on the wing
no one knows your devil's name
evil wicked mean and fast

NOCTURNE

Even though there are footmarks on her skin
and the doctors say that she is getting
more unstable, more unpredictable
by the month — she may even be frigid
to her core — there she goes, still hanging out
in her old haunts: I can see her tonight
through the bare branches of a leafless tree.

And in the darkness the frogs make noises
louder than trucks on the distant highway.

NEW ENGLAND GRAVEYARD INVADED BY TREES

        Martha Rogers lies alone
        underneath a red sandstone,
        eighteen ten to sixty-five
        were the years she was alive.

        On evenings, did she walk this path?
        her gingham dress floating over the pebbles,
                silk ribbons flying,
                slender arms, fingers
                throwing back her hair —
who held her breasts beneath the flowering dogwood?
                squeezed a nipple in Maytime?

        Silver birch the eye deceives,
        nature hides the dead with leaves,
        but *her* stone stands, Lord be praised,
        others fallen, names erased.

        The spirit turns upon the dust:
as imperceptibly as grief the summer lapsed away —
                a great hope fell,
                you heard no noise,
                the ruin was within:
as from the earth the light balloon asks nothing but release,
                she laid her docile crescent down.

        The trees and I gather round,
        point our faces at the ground,
        I ask one, he shakes his head,
        all we know is that she's dead.

SNOWSCAPE

The longboned rock has stuck its knees and elbows through
a tattered coat of snow on the western Catskills.
Across the whitened chamber of a large hollow
the brambles burst like particle trajectories.
A randoming flake negotiates a landing.

Sound bounces down into the valley, hound and dove.
A red plastic bucket leans half sunk in a drift.
Rubber boots stand on a doorstep. At one hill farm
a Ford has buried its nose in a soft hillside,
three cars nuzzle like pups on a great white udder.

PEACEABLE KINGDOM

I shake ants from a paper cup
before throwing it on the fire,
which may be out

of respect for natural things,
a nod to whatever powers
reign over campsites in darkness —
may be watching

as ants forage among grass stems.
The chemical-impregnated
paper cup ignites in a flare

that illuminates a woman's
face and arms and hands and ankles.
It may be her

presence that arouses in me
the notion to preserve ant lives
beneath limbs and resinous scales
of the mammoth evergreen trees.

EQUINOX

Fat man in a baseball cap
bottle of beer in his hand
looks up at the starry sky
two a.m. in the darkness
alone in a trailer camp.

Caught in the beam of my light
he gives me an alibi:
think this is the Big Dipper?
know if that is the North Star?

Nobody wants to seem weird
voiceless caught gazing at stars.

OLD PEOPLE WANDERING

Their biological work is done,
they have no more orders for the young,
now they pass like tourists through the place
where they were begotten and begot
in turn, and like tourists often do
they know more of local history
than the people who now run the show

TO MY DAUGHTER

Do you remember the turtle? I've forgotten
his name. His shell was cracked when we found him on the road
by the lake. Some Massachusetts kid had run his truck
over him. It was October and we took him
home with us to the city. He spent the winter
on a rock in a fish tank in a heated
apartment. We bought him tiny goldfish to eat.
He preferred tuna salad on a piece of lettuce.
The goldfish grew and became too big for him
to eat. Then they needed a fish tank of their own.
The following spring, on an April morning,
we returned the turtle to the lake and watched him swim.
We kept the tank of goldfish for several years.
Zachary was the snake. What was the turtle's name?

NEWLYWEDS

The newlyweds floated face down
in about three feet of water
      off Cape Cod.

They watched life on the sandy floor —
shrimps and big red starfish — through their
      snorkel masks.

She saw a small body and long
legs with weed growing on them — a
      spider crab.

It scuttled beneath her and she
jumped up and pulled the mask off her
      face and screamed.

God! It almost touched me! she wailed.
As they saw her clutch herself and
      wade ashore

swimmers abandoned the water
and lifeguards eyed the surface for
      telltale fins.

YOU CANOE

and stop
on a lake top
and look down into the clear deeps
as far as sunlight penetrates
and see
innumerable
struggling things
and little fish looking up at you
and you keep still
so long
the birds hidden in the shoreline trees
forget you are alive and go back
to doing the things they were doing
before you arrived

AFLOAT

High overhead I heard the traffic on the bridge
indistinctly through the fog but I saw nothing.

Ahab at the wheel of his big white motor yacht
his wife and guests below were playing cards.

He said what he was doing had less risk
than anchoring and waiting for the fog to thin

and chance being hit. Besides he had to appear
in court tomorrow morning or find a reason

the judge would accept. A bell pealed clearly
through absorbent fog its buoy lifted

on our wake. Behind us and out to sea
a groaner called like a sleepy walrus.

Ahab peered ahead. I poured scotch on rocks.
He had radar, charts, satellite positioning.

I said I'd stand in the prow and wave if I saw
anything. I did not expect to sight

the side of a house and some coniferous trees
directly in our path. Through its picture window

I saw mom, pop and two kids watch television
from a couch and turn their faces in unison

to look at us. Ahab swung the craft to starboard
of the tiny island with its lone summer house

and we were gone from their window view in moments
vanished into atmospheric interference.

PISSARRO IN MASSACHUSETTS

In the Sterling and Francine Clark Art Institute
near Williamstown in Massachusetts (the Berkshires)
you can see how Camille Pissarro liked to paint
industry's incursions into agriculture —
chimneys belching puffy smoke from small factories
that are quite plainly making only small headway
against the pasturelands festooned with wildflowers.

From Mount Greylock's nearby summit, the highest point
in Massachusetts, once walked by Mr. Thoreau,
      you can look down at a wooded valley
      and see an old New England mill town
      rest on its river, the waterwheels gone,
      the tall redbrick factory chimneys
           as empty as church spires.

      Trees, once downed by the sweating Puritans,
      have invaded the fields and now stand tall
in the smokeless air of the picturesque valley.

Would Pissarro jump on a bus to New York
      today or would he stay to watch
           on goldenrod
      brown velvet bordered by blue beads
           mourning cloaks
              open their wings?

STANLEY KUNITZ GARDENING

Reading things in his early nineties
Stanley Kunitz mentioned gardening,
how he found it difficult to bend
at his age, how he no longer worked
on his knees for any length of time.

He solved these problems by lying down
among the plants he needed to tend
and working in a prone position.

All went well until an ambulance
arrived one day and paramedics
held and secured him on a stretcher.

When Kunitz claimed that nothing was wrong
the emergency room doctor said,
 "You were reported lying face down
in flowers, twitching convulsively."
"I was weeding," the poet explained.

WINTER FIELD

A small dark figure
walks across
a distant snowy field

Snow is visible
through the trees
leafless on the ditches

The small dark figure
moves slowly
across the distant field

TOUR

Only rarely out of Connecticut,
she'd visit four European cities
in eight days with two friends and backpacking
stay in hostels. On her return, I asked
how much she liked Amsterdam. Great, with all
the Australian guys she met. Brussels too
and Paris. London was best. Some real
cool Australian guys at the hostel there.

PHOTO OPPORTUNITY

City women see an old bull moose
eating grass by the side of the road,
leave their car and approach real slow

so as not to frighten him. You first,
I'll take your picture, and then my turn.
The other picks some flowers she thinks

the moose might like to chew and holds them
out to him as she gets near. She says,
He's almost twice as big as our car.

He's smiling, the photo shooter claims
and she takes a shot. A state trooper
eases to a halt at a distance.

Once out of his car, he draws his gun.
Don't turn around, he calls. Walk backward
to the sound of my voice. They both turn

and stare. OK, he says, move slowly
toward me. They ask, What did we do?
They do not put their hands in the air.

You crazy bitches want to have me
killed? A driver passing phoned on this.
Jump in your car and get out of here.

Yes, the moose gazes into the lens
with what could be called a smile, and next
to his head a woman waves her hand.

2

SAVANNAH IN JULY

Mosquitoes bite downtown, wet and heavy air
feeds Spanish moss that droops off live oak branches
on period squares, each graced with monuments:

John Wesley in Episcopalian garb,
a railroadman, a general and his son,
an Indian who befriended Englishmen

and so on. The ornate bandstand in one square
repeated in another, or so I think
until I notice the same wino in it.

An old woman smiles at the pink-flowered trees,
the name of which she cannot recall just now,
but what a mess they make, petals everywhere.

HEADSTONES WITH
AN IRISH NAME

Beneath Savannah myrtle
two stones independent stand
side by side, identical
but for symbols carved on top:
hers a papist IHS,
a masonic compass, his.

ALLIGATOR

noses along
the water top

knobby body
parts the lilies

its tail moving
from side to side

reptile propelled
in no hurry

EGRETS

Egrets on the estuary elegantly
            in white-detergent plumes pick their way
     on tidal mud flats.

Dozens rise brilliantly white against the dark clouds
            their intensity of whiteness
     a forecast of rain.

The fashions changed in ladies' hats and boas
            the scatter guns of plume hunters
     hang in museums.

A lone egret stands long-legged on a cow's rump
            the cow seems glad of the company
     twitching its ears at flies.

As the cow moves through the meadow grass the egret
            runs alongside gobbling insects
     raised by the cow's hooves.

The earth is being scraped free of grass and trees
            to widen a Georgia road
     cars roll slowly by.

     Frantic egrets stab
            worms in the dirt and run in flocks
inches from the flattening tracks of heavy machines.

HOTHOUSE GERANIUMS

    turn the tornado
    funnel pink

DISTANT FUNNEL

The road straight to the horizon,
a known number of miles away
when you're at sea. The tornado —
this is deep inland — is slightly
left of the road and wider than
both lanes, probably impressive
in size. Its anvil cloud points right.
On the left hand side there's blue sky,
making the amber atmosphere
look sinister. You know your end
will not be as pretty as this.

PORTAVANT INDIAN MOUND

A mound of shell midden by the seashore,
tallest in Tampa Bay and area,
sprouting trees and ferns, by the mangrove edge
of the river mouth, topped by a fallen
chimney and concrete rainwater cistern.
Two interrupted rows of royal palms
line a path of broken shells to water.

Indians made a deliberate mound.
The man who built the vanished house on top
was loosed from a Union jail. His daughter
was born in this pioneer place. They moved.
A man whose name is now misspelled built the
cistern and grew citrus trees, two of which
still fruit. Then came the loving pair who set
the two wandering lines of royal palms
down to water, and they repaired the house.
She swam to rescue him and both here drowned
in the mouth of the Manatee river.

A boardwalk protects the mound. The state cuts
invasive trees to help native species.

JEFF CLIMBS OUT AND WALKS AWAY

In the Budweiser Shootout
at Daytona Beach with three
laps to go Jeff Gordon is
blocked by Kyle Bush and Gordon
taps his left rear fender and
pushes Bush off the track but
loses control, goes sideways,
gets hit and lifted into
the air, flips, end over end
to the grass inside the track
and instead of settling down
the car bucks, shudders and jumps
like a fish hung on a line,
expends the stored energy
you hear about in physics
before flopping on its roof,
only its wheels still moving

ALABAMA, 1964

There were things I still
did not understand.

Like all diners
where buses stopped
on interstates
it was integrated.

One end however
looked segregated.

I asked the black man
eating next to me
at the counter,
"Why do they eat down there?"

A white counterman
stood opposite me.

"This one," he said,
pointing to the black man
sitting next to me,
"leaves around here
on the bus with you.
Those ones," he said,
pointing to the black men
crowded at the end
of the diner,
"live around here
after dark."

"Now I know," I said.

"Now you know,"
he confirmed, evenly.

PERENNIAL WEED

    Beneath the concrete surface
lies a reinforcing mesh of steel.

    On the smooth cheek of concrete
        only mold can cling,

    black and green molds whose fingers
insinuate between the particles.

    Mold can do nothing to lift
my spirits, unlike an unnamed plant

    squirting out of a deep crack
that given time will shoulder aside

    the massive blocks oppressing
        its stem and its roots.

EASTERN SHORE

Three men working on a county road,
    they would know.
But they didn't, they said they never
heard of the house we were looking for.
I showed them the map in the guidebook,
the old house must be near where we stood.
    They shook their heads.
Then they looked at the guidebook's cover,
a WPA travel guide
published in the late 1930s.
One said, You're on the wrong county road,
they changed the route numbers years ago.
    Another said,
I know now which house you're looking for,
it burned down long before I was born.
More than forty years ago, I guessed.
The two saw things that made them laugh as
    they turned pages.
The third man quietly looked at us.

3

INDIAN GUIDE

Walpole Island Ojibwa,
Woody slapped at the flies and said how
he worked as a guide and took
groups of Ford executives hunting.

The men from Detroit and he
flew far north one time in a floatplane,
touched down on a pine-edged lake
and trekked into the trackless forest.

Woody had never before
been in a genuine wilderness.

They wandered for hours, told jokes
and had a very good time in there —
shot at anything that moved.

The sun got low ... they looked at Woody
and Woody looked back at them.

Then it dawned on him they thought of him
as instinctive pathfinder
who, no matter how spun, would point home.

He raised a palm to show peace
and said, with wooden face, Follow me.

Although they saw the humor
they believed and followed. On his part
Woody realized he had
marked the landmarks as they expected.

HIS UNCLE

He remembered leaving wild berries outside the door
and hoping the old man would think ghosts had left them there
and dragging by its tail a whole salmon as a gift
and hearing the rambling stories of the potlatch times
when the old man's father saw the things he told his son.

This was while he was still a boy and called the old man
uncle although not sure he was his father's brother —
if he was he was very much older and never,
unlike them, left the coastal village of their people
and this was where the anthropologists talked with him.

That was while the old man was still a middling young man,
between the two world wars, and people said about him
he was telling the anthropologists things about
their people that these strangers should not be told about
and was making up stories for pay that were not true.

Forever after the old man only laughed and said
that in those days he drank a lot and spent the money
on whiskey and beer, and often had no idea
what he had said but could remember having mixed up
secret things about their people with stuff he made up.

The people of older generations, when they heard
the things written by anthropologists about them,
laughed when the old man's jokes and lies and imaginings
took over from real true things about their people,
concealing things so that they alone knew which were which.

When they heard in the city that the old man had died
his father left a plate of food in their flower bed
in case his journeying spirit came by to bid them
farewell, and his younger sisters and brothers grew still
the next morning when they saw that the plate was licked clean.

FAMILY VISIT

On a sailboat bobbing on a choppy bay
a rope is making a metallic
sound against the aluminum mast,
which brings me back to the early morning hours,
years ago, on a wood porch attached
to a mobile home, on a stifling humid
night on an Ontario reservation.
I had gone to sleep at ten p.m.,
like everyone else. I stood outside at four
smoking and looking up at the stars
in total darkness, total silence.

A thing making that metallic sound
passed where I knew the dirt road to be,
a dozen yards from me in darkness —
I heard no other sound but clanking
of rope on an aluminum mast
on a choppy bay on this windless
stifling night in a place at least fifty miles
from the nearest standing body of water.
I thought of owls, nighthawks and nightjars,
nocturnal birds swooping low over the dirt
roads, making that peculiar sound.

At breakfast with my wife's family
next morning I asked what might have made
the metallic sound that had passed up
and down the dirt road several times
before fading. This caused a silence
at the long table. What had the white man (me)
done now? An elderly cousin said
my wife's grandfather rode a sled that was pulled
by a horse. It was silent and fast
over snow, and so to give warning
he tied a cowbell to the harness.

It was true we had searched for his grave
the day before in the neglected graveyard
among fallen trees and heavy brush.
At the place, when she was still a child,
my wife half remembered he was laid,
she placed chocolate and cigarettes
and I poured whiskey. Now he had visited —
and I had not woken her in time,
a new grievance added to her store,
because somehow she knew he would not come back
again, lost now to her forever.

LAKE SHORE

Touched by the wind in odd patches of ripples,
the lake is calm, the opposite shore hazy.

On the grass bank a man is supine, hat dropped
over his face. Beside him a woman reads,

showing her arms to the sun. A line stretches
taut from a rod to the lake depths. The woman

looks up. A thing slaps in the grass at my feet,
making me jump — a gasping silver-scaled fish.

HONEYBEES WALK

Honeybees walk on the maple leaves
eating the leaf pores' sweat of sugar

Bursts of day-flying forester moths
hit the wall's virginia creeper

Their deposited eggs outnumber
the shares traded on the stock exchange

The strong yen makes some Japanese sad
about American bonds they own

They are startled by the metal clang
the green bell in the temple garden

PHANTOM INFANT

Weeks before the birth
of her first baby,
she looked down and saw
a phantom infant
gazing up at her
with his father's eyes.

Then he smiled at her,
his sharp little teeth
stood in even rows,
and he said, Feed me.

MARINER LOST

A weekend mariner,
among his friends a font
of navigational lore,
clutches an encrusted plank
beneath a wave the size of Fuji,
in the shimmering depths of which
a finned leviathan
sports an appraising eye.

Through broken cumulonimbus
a shaft of light
bathes the mariner's face.

Mistaking it for
a helicopter's
air-sea rescue beam,
the mariner looks up and sees,
trident upright,
Neptune smile.

NEED

It was when you caught
the rat in the trap
and threw the wire cage
in water
to drown the beast

the rat in the trap
used its head
to force apart the wires
and swam to gasp in air.

It's when you can't open
a painkiller bottle's
childproof top
and you tear apart
its clear plastic skin.

WALK

She walked around the big pond
in the Luxembourg Gardens
feeling she was being followed

quickening her steps and almost
catching a fleeting movement
out of the corner of her eye.

She saw she was being followed —
a golden shoal of foot-long fish
swam in formation behind her

and when she stopped they waited
to be fed milling about
orangely in the green water.

She thought about the friend who lived
in Churchill on Hudson Bay
who had no fear of polar bears

but hated to be followed
with her dogs at the water's edge
by a pod of killer whales.

CRAWL

For fear they hide spiders
no pictures on the wall.

An octagonal home
with no deep dark corners
in which devils can hide.

A scorpion may spend
the night inside a shoe.

A guest wakes in the dark
to feel the brush of fur
upon her skin and shrieks.

The kitten runs in fright.

A SLIGHT EDGE

1
Although there's a sheer
drop of twenty feet
on the wall's far side,
coils of razor wire
assure the tenants

2
His mind so vicious
remarks so cutting

some day he will climb
a water tower

shout down at passersby
while they shoot up at him

3
A taxi brakes to a halt
by the river, the driver
gets out fast and runs away.

Perhaps I should take cover.

He turns around and runs back,
looks upward, stretches, breathes deep,
sits inside and drives away.

4
The bright white ameba core
delicate pink aureole
of an exploding missile
exist a millisecond

a flower that opens up
the innards of a city

MOONS

1
In binoculars
the full moon
orange through
city haze
shows what an omelette
should look like
when perfectly cooked

2
Triton, moon
of Neptune,
small, bright,
cold, pink

SAY IT WITH FLOWERS

Who knows whose idea it was
to sink tulip bulbs at Christmas
at random in the calm acres
of lawn that stretched before the house.

The absent owner was a hailed
authority on Henry James.

According to the photograph
the petals would be all one kind —
jagged bands of yellow, black, red,
a comic art depiction of
hot rod or funny car exhaust.

In spring, in the early morning,
his wife phoned to say that he was
thrashing the blossoms with his cane.

PEN NAME

If you write novels
with action heroes
expect some letters
from mail box numbers
in small towns near large
penitentiaries.

A guy who wrote me
about a combat
book I did was sure
I must have served in
the same unit he
did unless of course

he was bullshitting.

HER WALK

    Her walk it goes
like she's unaware.

    The traffic grows
as the drivers stare.

    Construction slows
as workers compare.

    She's wearing clothes.
Imagine her bare.

EARLY MORNING BAUDELAIRE

You know how birds scream their heads off when you
are trying to get a little shuteye
in the morning. I suggest that next time
you find yourself beneath a spreading tree
before the dawn's first light, take the trouble
to blow cigarette smoke into the leaves
above you to irritate avian
bronchioles. And before you leave, be sure
to shake the branches where you think they sleep.

CLOUDS

In these parts you don't often see
big puffy clouds sail one by one
across the blue sky, out of shape
clouds that just haven't looked after
their cumulous bodies – not mist
or wisps elongated along
a globally curved isotherm.

These clouds float like comforting thoughts
and bulge like overstuffed armchairs
against the thin atmospheric
blue of empty space above us.

LANCASTER COUNTY PUT-DOWN

I slowed my car when I saw
an Amish man wait to cross
the narrow road to a yard
and left him plenty of time
but he continued to wait
and I stopped so we could see
what he looked like while he crossed
in his beard, straw hat and boots
and halfway across the road
he raised up his arms and danced
to the gate that he then closed
behind him and walked the yard

GOING BACK

      I walked around the town
on streets familiar from other days
but I saw no faces my eyes had longed to see,
no one on the sidewalks, entering stores,
leaving buildings or sitting in a coffee shop.

      I do not say it was
now a horror film alternative town
populated by a variant human form.
I do not even say I did not see
anyone I knew – only none I wanted to.

LOOKING FOR WALTER

I will not say Walter had disappeared.
I hadn't heard from him in many months
and his friends had not met or talked to him,
but too soon to claim he had disappeared.

On the turnpike upstate one day we took
the exit for the town in which he lived.
I had come here once before for an hour
and remembered where his yellow house stood,
carpenter gothic with gingerbread trim
like all homes in this web of empty streets.
Where the house had stood a wire fence enclosed
an area of finely broken stone.
I asked someone, What happened to the house?
That's always been here, she said, though the fence
looked recently erected. Nobody
knew Walter – at least that was what they said.

A long-tooth bartender poured us draft beer.
No one there admitted knowing Walter.
Person by person, insidiously,
the undead had taken over the town.
Walter had resisted friendly offers.
By now no untainted people remained.
Missionaries were already moving
in twos and threes to other local towns.
No one said a word. The beer tasted strange.
Would we escape this place in human form?

4

BEFORE INTERCONTINENTAL MISSILES

The early warning radars strung inside
the Arctic Circle could provide three hours
to hide yourself from nuclear bombers
approaching America by the Pole.
A cousin spent four winter months in an

aluminum igloo packed with radar,
radio transmitters, generators,
fuel and supplies, alone because one
person could handle it better than two.
He had heat and food and plenty to do,

although he did not need to keep alert
for overflying Soviet aircraft
since long-distance radio transmission
of radar would waken America.
Snow fell, wind howled, daylight lasted an hour,

he heard taps on the igloo's metal skin
and he thought it might be a polar bear
but when he heard a shout he raised the hatch.
The Eskimo fed his dog team and drank
Coca Cola, smoked, chatted, slept a while

and left. My cousin could talk anytime
for any length by radio, mostly
to women, who sometimes cleverly placed
questions about his emotional state.
A woman with a velvet voice asked if

it had occurred to him the Eskimo
might only be a hallucination –
after all he was in a snowy waste,
below zero, about two hundred miles
from the nearest human settlement, in

an almost invisible white igloo.
He wondered what he might say after one
arrived with a dog pack a week later
and claimed he would only stop long enough
for a Coke, a smoke and to feed his dogs.

The skies remained clear of attacking craft
and minute by minute the days lengthened.
One, sometimes two, came almost every week.
He asked but never learned from where they came
and they never said where they were going.

RUBY BEACH

After the sun, like egg yolk
separating from albumin,
slips over the edge
of the Pacific rim,
from the beach we climb
the forest path
on which the huge yellow
slugs with black spots
are easier to avoid
in fading light
than dark red ones
glistening like cabernet

IMPRESSION

Had Monet a field
of multicolored
Washington dahlias
the man would have chucked
his pond and lilies.

Mendel would have traded
sweet peas, and Darwin his
Galapagos finches.

Vincent would have put
his peaceful absinthe
on the zinc counter
and swung at Gauguin.

FRIDAY

This morning I woke alone,
empty and full of fear.

What I do now, I decided,
must not be dictated by my fear.

Resisting the urge to lose myself
in work, I reached instead

for my guitar and played
the few tunes I play tolerably.

As I hung the instrument back
on the nail in my bedroom wall,

sunlight hit the bare wood floor.

URBAN PROBLEM

An old friend in Oakland
lives in a part of town
that's getting gentrified.

He looks back on the time
when nightly gunfire kept
the upwardly mobile
a neighborly distance.

Now he ponders maybe
handing out blanks to friends.

PONDEROSA

Ponderosa on a slope
of university grass
on a San Francisco hill,
the place they agreed to meet
if catastrophe occurs,
when his highrise office shakes
its contents into the streets,
when she drops her things and runs,
people flailing everywhere,
they will come to meet beneath
this big pine tree on this hill

ELEPHANT SEALS IN CALIFORNIA

1
No appointment in my name
to visit elephant seals.

Reservations must be made
at least a week in advance.

This is now the second year
I am being turned away.

2
Rangers closely supervise
small numbers of visitors

to keep them from disturbing
the breeding elephant seals

on an isolated beach
in protected wilderness.

3
Going south? a ranger asks.
Opposite the entrance gate

to the Hearst estate, you'll see
a colony overflow

just doing their thing roadside.
You don't have to leave your car.

4
Scarred, a bull elephant seal
guards his females on the beach.

Rising high on front flippers,
he points his snout in the air.

He makes a noise like water
circling down a metal drain.

HOME AND CASTLE

When I mentioned how Hearst in his castle
had a strict code of behavior for guests
and how you knew you had been caught and judged
when a chambermaid next morning unasked
began to pack your bags
                                      a friend announced
anyone who visits her apartment
and steps out of line is out the door
no time lost and good for Mr. Hearst
the man knew how to run a castle

THEY HUNT TO EAT

1
At Ojai a coyote waits
in darkness in long grass by a dirt road
waits for our approaching headlights
to illuminate creatures scurrying
and when we stop he slinks away
I think not pleased we understand his game

2
The falcon knows the flakes of snow
break up his image in the eyes
of pigeons on the empty street
and glides on windswept pointed wings
at speed above the traffic lights
unseen until it is too late

BODYGUARD

Bodyguard to the stars
might seem an easy way
to make a buck, with sex
and other perks maybe.

Beautiful, ultra fit,
scampering among the
rocks west of Malibu,
trailed by her bodyguard ...

Flushed, overweight, a cop
off duty, flat-footed,
where she goes there he goes
and dreams of criminals.

TOOK A LOOK

He gave her the binoculars
to watch brown pelicans gliding
over Malibu onshore kelp.

She said, I think that surfer there
acts in a television show.

RAPPER GUNNED DOWN AT UPSCALE MALL

Dolla might have liked the posturing mockingbird
        perched on a cypress tip
only a few miles away from the Westside mall,
bending its evergreen apex under his weight
and loudly singing his territorial song:
the notes and phrases repeated up to six times,
his tone varied, vocabulary extensive.

Dolla arrived at LAX early that day
and he went with friends to the Beverly Center.
        He was shot in the head
near the La Cienega Boulevard entrance.
The LAPD later detained a man who
allegedly drove from the mall to LAX
in a rented silver Mercedes SUV.

The mockingbird sings in darkness, after midnight,
his impulse triggered perhaps by a backyard light
lighted up by a time-control switch, and he sings
before dawn in anticipation of the day
        and he sings all the day
with a vehemence that might exhaust a rapper,
answered by rivals on nearby eminences.

DELTA FLIGHT 708

In the seat in front of me
a guy in baseball cap and fancy audio gear
    pulls down the window shade and
        I push it up.

He claims the light interferes
with viewing his seat-back screen and there's nothing for me
    to see out the plane window
        except some clouds.

I say he'd be better off
watching clouds than Britney Spears videos, which hits hard.
    Come on, I wasn't watching
        no Britney Spears,

he insists, to which I say,
I'm not criticizing you, it's none of my business
    what you watch. He seems to sink
        low in his seat.

In a while I hear him say,
Anyway there are no Britney Spears videos here.
    No more talk of window shades.
        I watch the clouds.

MANDATORY EVACUATION AT 3 A.M.

      Mandatory evacuation,
the sheriff's deputy declares. You need to get
      your things together and get
           out of here.

      The wind has changed, and nothing can hold
wind-driven flames. If they come off the mountainside
      they will burn every one of
           these houses.

      I get my things together and load
the car. The sheriff's men cannot force me to leave.
      The woman who lives next door
           wonders if

      I have any kind of fishing net.
She has collected her five cats and dog but she
      will not leave her fish behind
           in the pond,

      not after hearing about the two
people who refused to leave and then were scalded
      while immersed in their backyard
           swimming pool.

THE LOS ANGELES BASIN STORY

The more we learn about
blind thrusts and seismic risk
and then witness a quake

California style
do its personal thing
the more we realize

the gods who make earthquakes
seem not to read any
books by seismologists

QUAKE

It was nine minutes to five, Pacific time,
by the moving hands on the face of my watch,

in strength a high two or a low three,
an earth tremor that caused no damage

but certainly one that we noticed
as we stood in the kitchen doorway,

a helicopter floating in the sky
bright red as a tropical fish,

on television white domestic geese
called swans by the voiceover,

and it was exactly nine minutes to five
by the count displayed on her digital watch.

PINKELPONKERS

In bed in the early morning hours
I hear tiny footsteps on the roof
much too light for raccoon or possum
or their babies – and squirrels are not
nocturnal and no way would rats or
big mice run on a roof in moonlight.

You'd never know what might be out there
so near the San Gabriel mountains.

While there seem to be many they sound
by their feet reassuringly small.

They keep scampering and skittering
above my head and I cannot sleep.

Pull on shirt and jeans and barefoot make
my way in darkness out the door and
snap on yard light and quickly look up.

I see a rooftop bare: nothing there.

Daylight tells its logical story:
a sweet gum's geometrical husks
with spikes and holes from seeds and with stems
attached lie wind scattered on the ground
and overfill the plastic gutter.

CAMINITO BRAVURA

Her heart went out to them,
the old pair in the building
she moved to, who took so long
even to leave the building,
assisting each other

and making sure they remembered
where they were going and had left
nothing behind, he holding the door open
for her, the door of the open-top

red Sixty-eight Mustang it took them
five minutes to get into, and three seconds
to burn rubber on the driveway

COYOTE

In one of the canyons that run through the city
of San Diego, earthen wall planted
with fire-inhibiting green succulents
next to our motel, as sunlight faded
into floodlights, a big coyote stood
motionless in a taxidermist pose.

We saw his black-tipped hairs and his calm yellow eyes
and when we stopped, no more than twenty feet away,
he shrugged invisibly and limped uphill,
perhaps an old male driven from the pack.

I was told he was waiting for a motel guest
to send out a little dog to relieve itself.

IN SEARCH OF POLYGAMISTS

I wanted to see polygamists
and left the bus at Salt Lake City.

It took only a short time to find
that Mormons looked much the same as me.

Then I saw people who seemed to fit
expectations of polygamy.

I followed them to another bus
and sat beside a man clothed like

Abraham Lincoln. The women could
have stepped out of an old Dutch painting.

He said I had made a big mistake
in thinking they were polygamists –

polygamists looked the same as me,
not them. At a lonely town, he asked

if I thought it strange that such a place
had so many large houses, each with

several independent doorways.
I said thank you and got off the bus.

I wanted to see polygamists,
even if they looked the same as me.

PROTEST

Was it in Colorado in the nineteen seventies
that an American Indian Movement activist
after the state-sanctioned and university-sponsored
archeological desecration of ancient graves
conducted a dig in a suburban cemetery?

A helper, committed in politics but by nature
a traditionalist, told the police they had arrived
exactly on time to stop an argument on whether
to walk away or dig all the way and repeat the crime.

ARIZONA AFTERNOON

The sky has the mild featureless blue
of an old woman's eyes. The white stucco
is blinding. Today the Superstition Mountains
look red and contorted. A kid on a bike
beyond the motel swimming pool
is selling drugs. He hasn't noticed how,
coiled and silent, the wall-mounted
camera monitors him.

MOGOLLON RIM

Atop
an inland cliff looking out on a sea of pines

      a dirt road
      wanders hour after hour
      from sunup to sundown

      merciless.
Thunderheads in full sail blow across the blue sky.

      Out here
      miles from anywhere
      in Arizona

      wilderness
hard to believe someone dumped industrial waste.

      I leave the car,
      feeling righteous
      indignation, and look

      all around me
at thousands of white plastic spheres smaller than golf balls.

      I pick one up:
      it is heavy and solid ice,
      a stone fallen minutes ago.

      Only now do
they begin to steam in the afternoon heat.

AN ANTHROPOLOGIST COMES FULL CIRCLE

    He went to Zuni Pueblo
to compile a Zuni dictionary
as a postgraduate student helper.

    Much of the time he listened
to the words and phrases of old people,
the few who spoke an old form of Zuni.

    Back in the nineteen twenties
before convenient mobile recording
he noted everything in fountain pen.

    In a year he discovered
before returning to his school back east
he had an aptitude for the language.

    He moved to other fields
in anthropology, had what is called
a long and distinguished teaching career.

    On retirement he thought back
to his early days in New Mexico
and drove there with his wife of many years

    who had been listening
to his stories about those early days
for many years and expected the worst.

    When he tried his Zuni
people smiled and understood what he said,
then several serious Zuni men

    came to their motel
to say the people had been listening,
word had gone around, they had come to hear

    he was one of the few
people who could still speak the old Zuni
and would he mind if they recorded him?

IN GALLUP

The train is moving at more
than twice your walking pace
and perhaps even faster.

Its long sad whistle warns that
this iron horse on its twin rails
is coming through the town.

A tall man who wears
a hat with an eagle feather
resting in the brim
saunters across the tracks.

I see him from where I have parked
outside a pawnshop
that sells museum-quality
squashblossom necklaces.

I watch as he walks
away from me into the path
of the oncoming train.

The diesel locomotive hauls
a quarter mile of freight cars and
sounds its long sad whistle
but is not slowing down.

The tall man ambles onward
across the pair of rails
on which the train is running.

No smokestack or cowcatcher,
the locomotive is plain
utilitarian
everyday anonymous.

He pays it no more heed
than if he stood in the path of
a charging armadillo.

The diesel's flat face
touches his buckskin coat as
he unhurriedly lifts a boot
over a glistening rail.

A bullfight crowd would yell
at the close pass between
train wheel and boot heel.

But no one watches – only me
invisible in my car
and the engineer who pulls
the long sad whistle.

LA JUNGLA

Renaldo walks in front. His machete
clears growth sufficiently for me to pass.
Things woken in the leaves will hopefully
sink venom-laden spikes or razor teeth
in him instead of me. I have no trust
he will allow this to happen to him
instead of me. In the greenish darkness
of dense vegetation, perhaps eyes move –
and sensors of approaching body heat.
Drops hang from points. Things absent do not screech.

The wood stock of the bolt-action rifle
is greasy with sweat and loose in my grasp.

On our way, Indian children threw stones
at our canoe. Egrets in white plumage
rose and flapped into the long green tunnel
ahead of us, over the caiman snouts
in black water. Iguanas perched on roots.

Renaldo walks ahead, his machete
slicing with a clean sound through succulent
stems. Life is abundant. Cheap. A big cat
could claw me to death in a few seconds
without my seeing its intent green eyes
or fur rippling on its muscled shoulders.

Let me return to the beach and cool my
body in its shark-infested waters.
It takes Renaldo only a minute
or so to find his dugout and outboard.

LONE SWIMMER

He had never seen a big hammerhead
so close inshore, he said. It must have been
looking for something. Luckily for you,
he said to me, you were not that something.

I felt the water pressure as it passed,
close and faster than a car, then again
the other way, not touching but bumping
me with water. The people on the beach,
I saw, were running and waving their arms.

This story ended at the line above
when someone said that I had got it wrong.
That shark may have been moving back and forth
for some time, warily coming nearer
to me with each pass, shy and unnoticed.

As I walked toward the beach, breaking lines
of surf between me and the hammerhead
may have confused the fish, which perhaps was
unaccustomed to eat so close inshore.

Bits and Pieces

DOGS

1
Cold February night,
the stars flashing like blades
in the empty black sky,
my head out the window
because I hear the cries
of birds migrating north —
they call again, but no,
it's a small dog yipping
somewhere in a highrise

2
The woman cuts the eye of meat
from the lamb chop. That ingested,
she picks up the bone and nibbles
daintily. She does not notice
how the dog bares its teeth and growls.
That bone's not hers. The dog catches
its master's eye and looks away.

3
Once years ago
living alone
without a phone
a Greek island
stone hideaway
when he was ill
the only way
he could get help
was put a note
in the collar
of the big dog
that came each day
for buttered toast

4
That dog is much too large to fit:
his hind legs and hind end and tail extend over one arm
his head over the other arm
the armchair
he's slept in since he was a pup

5
Please make way
for the small dog
with a long stick
in its mouth

INSECTS

1
She slapped her hand against her skin
      on biting midges.
I said, You are being attacked
      by tiny vampires,
but they are psychological –
      there is nothing there.
And then I felt them biting me.

2
Let me say I think that fly was right
not to try to scratch its thigh in flight
but to land upon a poet's hand
to rub one leg against another

3
Say goodbye to him, the woman said
      to the little girl in the park
           stroking a caterpillar on a leaf

4
Above each gas jet
a grillwork spider

5
Fruitflies running on
a cantaloupe rind
in a plastic bag
can walk through the knot

6
On top of a page
a painterly swirl of blood
tail to a comet
of broken mosquito legs

7
Beware, avoid that cobweb
with your new feather duster.
As long as the web remains
so does the spider. Destroy
the web, you free the spider.

8
Instead of killing him
you lower the window
to free the country fly
and say you hope he finds
his folks again.

I remind you
that we have driven miles
since he first flew inside
and might have driven back
before releasing him.

CATS

1
A light bulb in a wire cage
illuminates the garden

Snowflakes flutter in its glare
downy cold-resistant moths

The sentry cat at window
claws against the pane at them

2
Yawns and shows its fangs
stretches lazily
pads to check its bowl

Clawed kitchen feline
panther of the couch
sleeping rug lion

A cat black by day
and chocolate brown
by evening lamplight

3
When she unlocked the door
her cat in his black fur
awoken from his sleep
all afternoon beneath
the dandruff blooming on
the asparagus fern
padded forth to greet her
with flowers in his hair

4
    Old
  at eighteen
  the cat knew
the girl of nine
now twenty-seven

Hadn't eaten
for days, he lay
  very still
  looked her way
    purred

5
Water pouring from a pitcher
down a plastic shower curtain
to floor of bath and then to drain
fascinates the cat, who watches
rivulets branch and multiply.

The pouring is monotonous
but watchers never see the same
thing twice. Its variety is
infinite, and its interest.

6
The cat asleep on wool
on the couch in the room
wakes and runs and then leaps
onto the tabletop
and drags a long-stemmed rose
by its head in his teeth
from the bowl because you've
answered the telephone

7
When cats running up and down
the hallway woke her in her
dream she knew that it was time
she gave a feline shelter

8
The cat watches
with half its face
and one green eye

9
To get her out of bed
exactly at six to
open a can of food
the cat sinks his teeth in
the plastic clock to make
it squeal and her to wake

10
The little girl held a mirror
to the mouth of the pregnant cat

looking down its throat
to see the kittens

11
Alive and thus unique
the cat basks in the sun

mindful of cats long gone
or homeless and hungry:

long-necked friends of Isis
beside the river Nile

or fierce on Celtic isle
a hermit's companion

or Rome's surreal groups
on Ancient Roman stones –

he's just baking his brains
making vitamin D

12
The cat sees me stare at
a paper sheet and comes
to investigate what
is there for me to see
something that he can not

13
A black cat
black cushion
its green eyes
when it yawns
its pink tongue

BIRDS

1
The pigeons hardly step
out of a runner's way
but take to wing when they
are being approached by
someone who walks slowly

2
O bird above, winging over
the earth on which I tread, how you
with little meatless boney legs
must look at me in awe and think:
If only I had feet and shoes

3
A thrush is stunned
on the earth amid leaves and vines.
He's eaten grapes
and the contents of his belly
a tiny fermentation vat
are too much for his bird-sized brain.
The thrush staggers,
looks as if he might throw up, he
doesn't feel like singing. He tilts
his head to fix an eye on me
and then he tries to hop away.

4
A stork flies, neck and legs outstretched,
high above a suspension bridge.

Headed north, it is bringing news
of birth among the chimneypots.

Folk north will watch it engineer
the bare sticks of domestic life.

5
A black two-headed eagle,
wings and claws outstretched,
on crimson background:
a flag that signals
Albania ain't foolin'

6
There are no eggs in Italy.
Italian hens give birth to live chicks.
This has had incalculable
consequences on the psyche
of Italians who think about it.
You'll find it's definitely not
something they want to talk about.

7
A heron shrieks
in moonlight

frightened by
its shadow

on the water

8
A winter morning
before dawn,
house sparrows
feeding by streetlight.

I'll get home
whistling my birdsongs,
try not to
fall over myself.

9
The heron
motionless

its reed legs
in water

outlasts the
memory
of fish that
dart over
the green stones

warned by its
landing splash

10
Birds of Hawaii:
the short-tailed albatross
is generally
silent at sea
but makes groaning sounds
on its breeding grounds

11
Born on top of a local highrise and trained to kill
        in city parks, a red-tailed hawk,
perched on a branch just out of reach, ignores the flashes
        of the telephone cameras.

It is a symbol of war, with massive beak and claws.
        Many pass with hardly a glance,
presuming, just suppose, it is a city pigeon
        reared on irradiated food.

12
The blue jays are screaming again, jumping
in frenzies from branch to branch and flicking
their blue crests in dreadful ultimatum,
all in one dysfunctional family.

They may die of stress-induced heart attacks
and fall to earth in crumpled blue feathers
or they're like the company boss who said,
I don't get ulcers from stress, I give them.

ULTRAVIOLET LIGHT FROM YOUNG STARS

1
What do you say, you say
if I could shoot geese
from my sofa, I would

2
Loved one, love done,
watch her tiptoe

3
Noodle soup and needle swap
no euthanasia for youth in Asia

4
Philadelphia, Alfio and Cirino:
their pictures on a stick stuck in the ground protects
a house from lava moving down slope on Etna

5
The kind of place
you shoot to kill
and watch a face
fall in the good
veal piccata

6
Levitation you might think
is not for heavy old men
who suffer lapses of faith

7
Why not do what they did with
the Hubble space telescope,
put yellow handles on it?

8
Me am in Bedlam

9
As they say in Haiti,
a fish trusts the water
and Is cooked in water

10
Keep on strutting
and crow, little brother

I'll hook the cooking pot
back on the wall

11
They found her guilty.
They had heard the choice
of a fashionably
thin icicle:

I would rather weep
in a Rolls-Royce
than be happy
on a bicycle.

ALMOST STILL LIFES

1
The pine moves
its big paws
and knocks snow
pads off its
green needles

2
Now it has abandoned flowers,
the cyclamen can concentrate
on growing big and foliate.

I guessed wrong about the flowers,
the cyclamen released eight more
pink-petaled rockets from its core.

3
A spray of yellow orchids
in midair
        like butterflies
flying in fixed formation

4
Flowers change, she said,
stems in vase, buds open,
petals spread, they curl,
hang on elegantly
as long as they can,
then fall dry and lightly
on the table top,
except chrysanthemums,
she said, which blandly
stare back at you until
you throw them out

5
The large bright purple irises
tossing their heads in the churchyard
don't say Christian humility

6
Schoolgirls in their own bright petals
have been picking bright red tulips
      around a tree
      as if plants were free.

A girl picks a tulip and looks
on it with a possessive smile
      before placing it
      beneath her coat.

Hours later the tulips are gone
except for a single flower,
      the last slice of cake
      no one will take.

7
Bougainvillea
like compassion
spilling over walls

8
A vase full, past their prime, in the apartment heat,
the lilies are splayed like empty banana skins
and each of the red-splotched orchids clings by one leg

9
The air was hot and they hung
loosely and every which way.
Now you see they stand upright
with petals held together:
proper little Dutch tulips.

CHILDREN

1
A friend in Scotland had
visitors for Christmas:
Australians whose child was
amazed by the snow but
who soon asked, When can we
go back to our planet?

2
The way your children can
look at you when you do
something they consider
age inappropriate

3
"She's gone to heaven," they told the boy
and tried to keep all the children out.

When he judged no one was listening
he whispered loudly to his mother,

"Nancy's not gone to heaven at all –
she's packed in a box in the next room."

4
A dozen children, no more than eight,
in school uniform, sit on the floor
of the Tate Britain beneath Three Studies for

Figures at the Base of a Crucifixion
by Francis Bacon, paintings in which
the anguished figures have lost human form.

What does the color red remind you of,
anyone? the woman sitting with them asks.
A boy raises his hand: Blood, miss. She says, Right!

5
As a child in the town of Oxford
in the long garden behind his home

Keith and friends played their games and ignored
Mr. Tolkien who lived next door

and complained of the noise that they made
while he scribbled in his garden shed

on Middle-earth's gnomes, elves and goblins
who could behave like noisy children

6
Wrinkled paper scraps
one blue and one pink
impaled together
on the writing tip
of a ballpoint pen
the child handed me —
a flower, he said

7
A child has picked a leaf
and now is looking up
inside a hanging branch

a gust of wind arrives

and the many hundred
brother and sister leaves
shake and loudly rattle

which makes the child alarmed

8
Rolling downhill fast,
rigidly clutching
the bike handlebars,
a small boy, eyes wide

9
   She could not balance well
   and walk upright. She did

a rapid locomotion on all fours
that would have made a spider proud on eight.

   Carefully held upright,
   a blue plastic bucket

received the cherry tomatoes she picked
as she crawled on the earth beneath the vines.

   She ignored tomatoes
   green and unripe and went

methodically after the fully red,

   knowing what she wanted,

cherrypicking the cherry tomatoes.

10
Try not to say this or that
   four-letter word
      the children might pick up and
         throw in your face

11
Pink for girls and blue for boys
and if I do not know which
a baby is, she repeats,
never call an infant *it*

12
Holding nine-day Lincoln,
a hundred in the shade.

Planes and helicopters
drop their fire retardants,
a San Gabriels blaze.

Hello, Los Angeles,
the infant Lincoln says.

BIZ PEOPLE

1
In his suit he
is bewildered
by his wife who
has embroidered
flowers inside
all his pockets

2
Busy, busy, busy …

All the time so busy
he hardly has time
to mentally process
clearly stated
data and information
directed his way.

He can only surmise
that some nonverbal
communications
zoom past him
like ground-to-air missiles
successfully eluded.

3
Believers rarely accept
new ideas on merit.

Economist Samuelson
has said knowledge advances
funeral by funeral.

4
The financier said
everything you need to know
about a country

you can see from a taxi
between the airport
and downtown hotel

5
He want to keep the things he got,
he want things to remain the same,
but he know that stability
is only a point on a curve
that go careening up and down,
never a horizontal line

6
For deals in nations overseas, Samuel Huntington has argued
that bribery can be the most effective way for businesses
to cut through red tape. The only thing worse than a society
with a rigid, overcentralized, dishonest bureaucracy
is one with a rigid, overcentralized, honest bureaucracy.

IT'S ALL REAL

1
No swiller of beer
or whiskey nipper
or champagne sipper
need be in pain here

2
A bulletproof convoy
of vehicles with strobes
flashing and last in line
an ambulance always
the possibility
of one dissenting vote

3
Only in New York City would a person say
on seeing a man with a golf bag on his back,
I wonder what musical instrument he plays

4
The tattoo wrapped around
her skinny upper arm
makes it hard to tell what
happens at the edges.

It will be easier
by far for you to see,
a woman friend remarks,
when she has gained some weight.

5
See how tonight the pictures on the wall
reflect in the big pane of window glass
and shrink and magnify and shrink again
as wind pushes and pulls the willing glass

6
A beetle rapidly climbs outside
      the square of window glass
its black silhouette against the sky
        gets larger as it moves
            its shape then grows and morphs
                to a helicopter

USA OK

1
Gravel is dragged
loudly by waves

the ocean is
clearing its throat

2
When one of the things unloaded from the floatplane
on a lake in Alaska was a thick mattress
they knew the new arrival knew a thing or two
and was at least no dreamer who might hope to scoop
for sleep a concavity to contain a hip

3
Early morning in a waiting place
in a small airport in the northwest
twenty to thirty rumpled people,
smeared with ash, asleep in splayed out clumps,
are emanating an aroma
of pine trees smoldering overnight

4
Her hears are awed of earring,
he said – or something like that.
I didn't disagree, I
said – something like that, I think.

5
A physician
said: Pick the six
unhealthiest
looking people
you see walking
these hospital
corridors and
most of them will
turn out to be
doctors like me

6
Wise men learn more from fools than fools from wise men
the fortune cookie in my Chinese takeout
tells me, but no instructions enclosed on how
to tell who is a wise man and who a fool –
too much of course to expect from takeout food

7
Have you ever noticed how
there's rarely news on weekends?

Weekends are when newsworthy
troublemakers stay at home
to torment their families.

8
I pocket my phone and gun
but cannot find my car keys
where I am sure I left them
though I could not swear to it

it's stuff like this that's going
to kill me I have no doubt
Some Simple Stupidity
will be the words on my stone

TEN POEMS

1
      A photograph she took
      through her highrise window
of a rainbow crossing the river

      a photograph in which
      a phantom image is
seen reflected in the window glass

      of her naked body

2
It's no secret big art objects
often are made by small people.

A question remains unanswered:
do short people write long poems?

3
Fireworks blossom overhead,
and in the dark above us
a sound of countless footsteps,
a sound of rushing water

4
The miniature aluminum stepladder, yes,
and the glass bowl with an incised tulip, yes again,
what they leave behind may say as much as what they take

5
So cold the air is clear
cold so that sounds carry
across Washington Square
cold so people hurry
except two women who
relaxed elegantly
in luxuriant fur
sit on a bench and who
smoke and talk in Russian

6
    If you can test
a statement's truth, it's science.
    And if not, it's
possibly philosophy.

7
When I suggested
the view of islands
and sea and mountains
might be mellowing
him from serpent to
bunny rabbit he
said he preferred to
think of himself as
crocodilian

8
They were surprised by the celebrities
who greeted her by name. They knew no one.
Him? On and off for seven years, she said.
Not a word from me that she was nurse at
a very expensive rehab clinic.

9
Early Friday afternoon
two young Lubavitcher men
near their truck and loudspeaker
politely asked me if I
was Jewish. Worse, I replied.
They stared. Irish Catholic.
One said, When I talk with him
the rabbi will laugh at that.

10
Are you willing to join
older Americans
in requiring Congress
to forward the New Year
from the stroke of midnight
to maybe around nine?

Ireland

1

1867: LAST SOUNDS

A few hundred from one village
left Rathlin Island in a famine.

In the evening, over the waves,
howling of dogs at the empty homes.

SCHOOLROOM INCIDENT

A nun and one
Hun dead alas
a long time gone
met on the thir-
teenth page of a
history book.

She bore to the
Hun twenty-one
undisciplined
laughing children
who all went home
when the bell rang
on page fifteen.

DRYAD

In the night
the spirit
of the oak
rustles on
the roadway
in her leaves

MOVING PARTS

1
Rattling grass
the sheep browse
in the sky

2
Afternoon quietly
lightning walks
      visiting
  and the sky bumps

A blackbird cock
dangles his song from the spiky branches

   Wheat stubble
      crackles in the air

Here
waiting for it now
  here
    yes here
the quick spatter on blackberry leaf and grass
   comes the rain

3
Round a stone
moves the stone
turns the stone
drowns a spider
  faster now
  easy moving
    down a hill
    up a stone
    round the stone
    drowns the stone

CELLS

Water supports
the transparent
the round the bulging
that pulse in
geometric defiance.

They may extend
a pseudopod
sting with acid
turn vermilion —
squirt, blind or glide
unappetizingly.

Lucky for the oak leaf
and the hen
this bag of tricks
under its own weight
like the whale
collapses on land.

&

It's hard to tell the difference
between male and female jellyfish.

Their babies metamorphose
into flowerlike cups.

The cup breaks up
into jellyfish.

&

Starfishes disseminate their oats
without a mate into the salty womb
of the ocean blue
great mother of sea urchins.

And each man likes to think of himself
as a highly active free-swimming type —
a spermatozoon
thinks any woman an egg.

&

The colony approached. It spoke:
You've changed quite a lot since you
were a fertilized egg.

RAIN

Ireland the rain is not falling
        out of the sky
                but dropping gently

FEAR OF VIKINGS
(*after the 9th century Irish*)

      The wind freezing,
snow whips into blonde curls
on top of the parked cars.

Tonight no wanderers
will roam the icy streets,
        their steel blades cold.

THERE AND THEN

Small tortoiseshell,
common blue,
speckled wood,
meadow brown,
peacock, brimstone ...
the butterflies
I may have seen,
lying with you
in stems of green,
the sky was blue

FROM ANOTHER TIME

Once upon a time an ornamental
pseudo pagoda golden-carp-filled lake
of a nineteenth century landowner

what was one time an ornamental lake
near the manor house that the rebels burned
now a blackened shell near the weed-choked lake

a heron's shriek in the gothic stillness
of these dim and greenly lit environs

this is all that is left of the old days,
remains of glory — listen! the sound of
an ancient gramophone's cracked tenor voice
among the trees leaning down to water
as the sun sets on an August evening
and the midges thicken beneath the elm,
an apparition thinly approaches,
his tweeds rustling, he casts an acorn here
and an acorn here and another there,
a retired admiral with pocketfuls,
so that the Empire will always have oak —
timber for ships of the Royal Navy

and down in the back where the berries are

there, on a fallen tree — a massive trunk
opulent in the grandeur of decay

stands a little fungus brightly colored
pink, vermilion or whatever you please

IRISH LANDSCAPE
WITH FIGURES

A chieftain joking
with his lady fair
passed on their horses
and to save his soul
he offered a coin
to unsmiling monks
who patiently hewed
resistant granite.

Melted and reworked
many times since then,
the gold of that coin
may be the metal
of the ring you wear.

And the granite cross
is where they left it.

SONG

One pleasant evening in the month of May
as I sat with worries gone far away
the color and shape of one of my shoes
reminded me of a bottle of booze.

What more shapely things can a man desire
than a girl and bottle and a guitar
and remember now not to miss your cues
when she shares with you a bottle of booze.

Keep your sob poems and your fancy art
my liver is hard and so is my heart
and even the blind man forgets the blues
when he swallows down a bottle of booze.

If I get drunk, well the money's my own —
if you don't like me, just leave me alone —
I'll turn up my digital radio
and I'll have music wherever I go.

2

A GALWAY STANDOFF

Water rattles the boulders
in wave action on the coast.
Salt in the wind devours steel.

A white cottage squats on rock,
back turned to the Atlantic,
its two little windows squint
even on calm summer days.
Nearby, an exurban house,
its naked picture windows
embrace the sea. Between these
two houses and the shoreline,
a field with walls of loose stones.

Beside some cows on grass lie
five hulks of abandoned cars.

These wrecks are country answer
to city insult. I've heard
they will not be moved until
city folk admit who's wrong.

One waits for apology,
one for steel to rust away.

BEDSIDE VISITOR

A window looking out on fields.
Framed prints of Daniel O'Connell,
Liberator, William Gladstone,
Home Rule for Ireland's champion,
brown-eyed Jesus baring His chest
to show His flaming crimson heart.
An old lady sits up in bed,
her cane in reach against a wall —
though it's beyond her now to leave
the bed without a helping hand.

She believes her grown up son is
her long-dead husband, his only
child is now her son and his wife
a nurse who is very lazy.

It's Halloween, near All Souls' Day.
The teenage boy, before he leaves,
wears a scarlet devil costume
and decides to visit Grandma.

The devil dances by her bed
as she screams and calls to Jesus,
Mary, Joseph and the angels
to help her in her hour of need.
The devil laughs, he grows careless.
The terrified old lady brings
her cane down hard upon his head.
Amazed at her strength, the devil
cowers beneath a rain of blows,
whimpers and rushes from the room.

And to this day she talks about
the time the devil tried to rape
her in her bed. The boy smiles now
that his bruises have disappeared.

ONE OF THE OLD SCHOOL

Joe Ryan of Raheen, a gentleman farmer,
each morning, before his breakfast, cut a flower,
a reddish or brownish respectable flower,
one to go with tweed, for his lapel buttonhole.

At race meetings, flower sellers accosted him.
"Ah, sure that's a poor dying thing to show the world,"
one would say and replace the inflorescence with
a bloom of greater size and more violent shade.

After the races, he would stop the car somewhere
to obtain, from someone's bed, another flower
that caught his eye as being clad more decently.

RIVER TEETH

A British Army career nurse, retired, Miss Sullivan
lived alone in a Dublin Bay suburban bungalow,
rooms hung with leathery shields, crossed spears, wood heads with bone eyes
and scores of bronze or copper bangles on a rawhide thong
my younger sisters were afraid to touch. The bangles came
from crocodile bellies stretched on equatorial mud,
reptiles hit by guns on a mission of sport and duty,
bangles round the upper arms of girls whose growing elbows
held them in place, girls who splashed while their mothers washed the clothes.

My sisters and I would pass the glass-fronted snakes and things
in the Reptile House at the zoo in order to gaze at
the grandfather crocodile, who snoozed in his long green pool,
who had yellow eyes and pretended to be deep asleep
and whose belly easily could have stored all four of us.

One afternoon a man walked inside the crocodile's lair.
We were there when it happened. I remember his cloth cap,
his cigarette, his rubber boots and the long-handled brush.
The beast was out of the water. We hardly dared to breathe.
The man threw suds from a bucket onto the floor and swept.
He looked at us, winked, grinned, threw suds on the crocodile's back
and scrubbed with the bristles its knobbly scales. We saw it purr
and left to wave at the snake that banged its head on the glass.

AIR SHOW

A layer of unbroken cloud
floated perhaps four hundred feet
above the faces of the crowd
in a field in County Dublin.

Stunt flyers in prop planes could work
at this low ceiling. With regrets
they had to cancel the star turn —
formation-flying NATO jets.

Although no rain fell upon us,
a spearhead of three olive drab
Yankee air force fighter bombers
swooped down and nearly touched our heads.

They had zeroed in and found us
beneath our protective layer
and showed us what we might have been —
sitting ducks at a county fair.

AN ANCIENT IRISH
SAINT'S FAREWELL

Before I go,
lay me softly
atop the grass,
I want to hear
a bird singing.

Lord, forgive me,
I find it hard
to leave behind
the land so green,
a finch singing.

A QUESTION

      The center of the universe,
        were it located deep beneath
the holy well outside St. Malachy's church,

      would coins that Mrs. Kearney dropped
        cause galaxies to heave and sway
beyond the icy light of far Arcturus?

PILGRIMS

Those who live year round with flowering trees and hummingbirds
think back on those they left behind and phone about the snow.

Light starved, knobbed and gnarled, frost and wind hurt, thin-fingered branches,
stark bare or, when it's appropriate, draped in chapel green,
erupt in chilled ecstasy — flowers tiny, astral, white.

Those of us who have thin, hard lives and labor through the ice
watch this mad flickering and swear that we will never show
our innards and fall wantonly to passing strangers' feet.

Springtime is brief, with all its painted birds and gaudy trees.

SIBYL

  Priests of a teaching order
  occupy the dower house
on what was once an Irish earl's estate.

  A mythological hag
  occupies a rock bower,
a prominent statue in the garden.

  A sibyl, a prophetess,
  an ironic gift no doubt
from one earl to his presiding mother.

  Devout, pious, mistaken
  in thinking her the Virgin,
people strew her feet with new cut flowers.

EXPLANATION

They gathered round her in a field
and every time one came too close
she clicked the flashbulb in its eyes.

It jerked its head and backed away.

So many photographs of cows.

HIGH NOON

On a narrow winding Irish road
    a little car
  travels slowly in front of mine.

    Its driver looks
fixedly ahead and is driving
    in the middle of the road.

    Two bikers pass
  wearing Hell's Angels colors
on Harley-Davidsons with Swedish plates.

But they cannot get by
the man in the middle of the road —
        on a sharp bend

he nearly puts them in a roadside ditch
      and judging by their gestures
           they seem impressed.

The biker with a long yellow beard
      and a metal skullcap
           that lacks its horns

        draws alongside
the slow-moving little car
in a death-defying maneuver.

The rider hammers on the car's hood
        with his ringed fist,
    looking back at the driver.

Although the little car almost wavers,
        it holds its ground
    in the middle of the road.

Having kicked a boot disgustedly
        against its door,
    Yellowbeard accelerates,

    followed by his boreal pal,
and as I pass too I glance inside
        at the driver.

He looks straight ahead, spectacles crooked,
        his small mouth tight,
    his face expressionless.

        Will he recount
these random and perplexing events
      to his wondering kin?

      Or have we encountered a man
        on his own turf
who does not cede an inch to strangers?

THIN AIR

You should know that as you climb them
even small mountains swell hugely.

On their slopes they develop rolls
of unwieldy surplus terrain.

After you mount each swelling rise
you see another higher up.

When at last you climb what you know
must surely be the final roll

another rises, and after
that, another and another.

You ask why this wavelike structure
was not visible from the ground,

why great professional climbers,
in their talk of cols, ice bridges,

sheer faces, crevasses, crampons,
don't mention this phenomenon.

And will your stopping and turning
so often to admire the view

take away from what you will feel
when you stand and gaze around you

at the very tip of the peak?

TWO SAYINGS OF MALACHY

The first to be treacherous
talks the most of loyalty.

Retrieve the philosopher
from underneath the table.

THE ONE UNREVILED

Vinegar in veins
crazy old woman
lingered forever
too sour to expire.

President's greeting
her hundredth birthday,
accused nuns in home
of telling her age.

Left all in her will
to niece who never
once paid a visit,
the one unreviled.

DONORE

Spring lambs are noisy,
constantly bleating,
butting their foreheads
toward the udders,
yelling plaintively
they can't find mother
and trying one ewe
after another.

Late one winter night,
flashlight battery
gone dead, in the dark
I grope for the switch
on the farmyard wall,
all silent and still —

feathery purr
of owl flight and
the bronchial cough
of an old dog fox
somewhere in the fields —

I find the switch
and flick the light
and see four hundred
pairs of eyes of
winter animals
huddled together,
silence of the sheep,
mute, sacrificial.

THREE SONGS FOR TIN WHISTLE

1
You know that he stands
there in the next room,
the antlered creature
with glassy brown eyes
who has poked his head
through the plaster wall

2
      Rain's a blessing
      here in Mayo —
the sheep get too waterlogged
to be blown over the cliffs

3
Scotsmen say she's quite a bitch
Nessie when she gets the itch
her skin as tough as leather
to roll around in heather

3

SHAPING UP THE GARDEN

He had come late
to gardening

after he got
too old for golf
which may be why

intricacies
involved in it
quite escaped him.

There were absolutes
called flowers and weeds.

It took him a while
to tell them apart.

Flowers had flowers,
weeds did not, though his
wife claimed otherwise.

One or the other:
you bore a flower
or you were a weed.

He took no prisoners.

SEAPOINT, DUBLIN

Walking out of the sea on a long summer evening
my father and my son my son aged five or six
my father eighty five or six their similar gait
is one of those traits that skip a generation.

Watching the two of them walk out of the sea
I light a cigarette in the concrete shelter
and having been in the water I shiver
the way people do home from America.

That your father and son walking out of the water?
a red-faced fellow says to me. It is I say.
Your old man often swims here late alone he says
and all the time I and others have to pull him out.

Constantly being rescued from drowning is not
a thing my father would thank anyone for or
acknowledge in any way as age and people
conspire against his doing the things he always does.

When I was five or six on a long summer evening
I went to the Bull Wall with a friend and his father
who swam out in an easy crawl turning his face
sideways to breathe while we splashed around on the steps.

We waited shivering long after darkness fell.
His worried mother sent a neighbor who brought us home.
I remember his father every time I watch
someone crawl across the water out to sea.

My father does the breast stroke fairly close to shore
and all the regulars seem to know what to expect.
I say nothing to my mother. It's late in August.
Soon enough the water will be too cold for swimming.

BECOMING NINETY

Becoming ninety, my father said:
Never live to be as old as me.
It's not a matter of aches and pains
or lack of strength or memory loss –
it bothers me most my friends have gone
and left me behind with all of you,
who do not see things the way we do.

A GENERATION MORE

"Your mother and I drank tea,"
the old woman said, "and watched you,
as a young girl, swing
in the apple tree at the end of the garden."

"That wasn't me you saw,"
the young woman said gently.
"That was my mother.
My grandmother was the one who drank tea with you."

SISTERS

Her dead sister paid her a visit
in her hospital room. She told her sister
if she was going to walk around
in her nightdress after three years in the grave
she could at least wear a cleaner one,
take a bath, maybe do something with her hair.
Things between them were going to be
not very much different in the afterlife.

DELUSION

She thought the government had made her home
a hospital room. That they had thrown away
her furniture and all the things she owned.
Everything was gone except herself
lying ill on a hospital bed.
Her family explained and she tried
to comprehend. But this had once been her home
and now look at it. Everything was gone
except herself. Her son said he had tried
to feed the fish in the pond but could not find
the pellets they ate. She said to look
for them in a round plastic container
on the third shelf by the pantry door
and that while he was at it he should
water the flowers but not water them
too much especially the orchids.
This hospital room had once been her home.
They had taken everything away.
Everything was gone now except herself.

HER LAST DAY

She was at home, where she wanted to be,
a window overlooking her garden.

A friend came for drinks, and they talked and smoked.
She did her nails an hour before she died.

FROM BEYOND

My mother was not I think the kind
I would expect to become a ghost.

All the same, the night I stayed alone
in her house, then a month empty since
her death, the thought did cross my mind that
we might see one another again.

That night, as I lay in bed, I heard
the sounds material makes as it
contracts with falling temperature
and sounds that might be door knobs turning,
doors closing, maybe loose boards yielding.

It was daylight when women's voices
woke me. They came from the back garden
beneath my upstairs bedroom window.
Half out of bed, I heard my name called
twice. I looked. The garden was empty.

The voice I heard call my name was not
my mother's, but a cousin's. Months back,
she found me sleeping at the airport,
having come to meet her, and woke me.

I recognized her voice and almost
immediately knew where I was.

4

IN THE EYE OF THE BEHOLDER

Amelia Earhart became
the first woman to fly solo
across the Atlantic.

She touched down on an Irish field
one afternoon and leaped
from the cockpit onto the grass.

The man who owned the land
had never seen a plane before.

He didn't seem taken aback
one had dropped from the sky
or surprised it held a female

pilot. But he had never seen
a woman wearing pants before.

She said he stared at that.

OUT OF SEASON

I had so fondly remembered this place, and here it is,
green and sullen, lichen like skin disease on its gray stones.

The little farmer on his giant tractor has no time
for city blow-ins with all their time and money to spend.

Wildflowers never grew here or it's the wrong time of year –
a month ago perhaps this place looked like I remember.

DOG AND SWALLOW

One after another, the swallows dived
above the sheepdog, which tried to ignore
and ignore, until in sudden frenzy

the dog threw itself aloft, snapped its teeth
and stayed in the air like Baryshnikov
among swooping fork-tailed ballerinas.

But this was not what the farm workers saw –
they all jeered the dog for biting into
emptiness, being fooled time after time.

One day a bird miscalculated and
the dog dropped the dead swallow at their feet.

Even motionless on grass, the chewed corpse
looked built for flight, its aerodynamic
curved-back wings formed a ritual spearhead.

The men applauded the slavering dog
that had seized its tormentor from thin air.

DOWN AT THE BOG

I met an old fellow down at the bog
who said he had just been chased by a frog,
a shiny green thing with damp-looking skin
that called him by name, with fast-throbbing chin,
with bulging eyes, in a voice he knew well
and long thought its owner safely in hell

GRACE AND RAINIER

Grace and Rainier of Monaco
chose the Curragh races

where she was welcomed home
and she smiled and twirled and charmed and he
was more or less ignored.

In a throwback to earlier times
Grace was lost in stardom.

Rainier looked genuinely pleased,
a prince who felt no jealousy
for the princess at his side.

BED AND BREAKFAST

Remember the saints and madonnas
in that awful room in County Cork?

You said their eyes followed every move
we made and insisted I get out
of bed to turn the pictures to the wall.

TRADERS NOW

We live as traders now.
Our way of life might not
surprise the Phoenicians,
veterans of countless
Mediterranean
Ancient World business trips,
who saw before their eyes
beliefs and customs change
from port to port. Like us
they were polite about
the local deities.
They needed all the help
they could get – if a coast
or town was protected
they made offerings to
the protector. Like them
we feel uncertain with
people who turn away
proffered gifts from the hands
of benevolent gods,
who respect only one
among many gods and
expect at voyage end
to dwell in Paradise,
some kind of promised place
where not even the great
Phoenicians navigate.

OLD PRIEST

An old priest with shaking fingers
who liked to stir about the words
in ancient books warned his pupils
of good and evil, always here.

Monks were the first to try Marxism
and found they needed an abbot,
he claimed, to judge those unready
for heavenly soul's heavy toil.

People today are weak to think,
he said, they can rely on plans
that fully depend on all hands
to pull evenly on the oars.

DEAD FISHERMEN

Drowned father, brother, son
no more kitchen voices,
menacing yet softer
than long-winged ocean birds'
loud wind-blown rasping cries.

You hear them call their names
above the wind and waves,
those who drowned, never found,
men whose ghosts haunt this coast,
calling eternally.

TELTOWN MARRIAGE

Ancient customs
gain relevance
when we find them

reasonable,
as with one old
Irish marriage.

Teltown marriage
lasted a year
and a day – could

then be ended
when the couple
stood back to back,

one facing north,
the other south,
and walked away.

They did not turn
at ten paces,
draw weapons on

one another
but walked onward,
not looking back.

GLENBUCK, COUNTY ANTRIM

These of course would not be the trees –
merely their sapling descendants –
in whose branches king Sweeney lived
some fourteen hundred years ago,
skin tattered by thorns into strips,
so many they looked like feathers,
though he could only jump from branch
to branch, not fly, with his fixed stare.

While he led his men in battle
his mind snapped like a hollow stem
and his body shook like green leaves.
Since then he has lived in tree tops
and rarely heeds the pleas of wife
to come home or brother's advice.
Look, he seems to recognize you.
Offer him a bottle of stout.

WEATHERWISE

1
In Maine people say
they have two seasons:
August and winter

2
In Galway they say
when people can see
the Aran Islands
it's a sign of rain

and when they can't see
the Aran Islands
already raining

OUTSIDE AN IRISH COUNTRY HOUSE

She might understand why you removed in
annoyance from the doorway of your home
the long granite rectangle upon which
equestriennes stood before they mounted
side-saddle for a day of foxhunting,
the black woman who wryly observes that
plantation houses and magnolias
are part of her cultural heritage

OUT OF THIS WORLD

    To hitchhike in Kerry
was not easy, not that drivers were unfriendly
but cars were few on roads with grass in the middle.

    You slept out of doors
when you were stranded, next to a stone wall.

As darkness silenced bleating goats and sheep,
even far from cliffs you could hear the waves

and you could think the gentle yellow lights
    that oil lamps cast
from scattered little cottage windows
were cabin lights of trawlers fishing
    a calm reach of sea.

    We heard music:
old men, one with an accordion,
one a banjo, a woman singing,
on kitchen chairs by a fire of sticks.

    We kept a distance,
listening, knowing they would stop
    if strangers heard them.

A score of children, some barely walking,
some nearly as old as us, girls and boys,
materialized out of the darkness.

    They tugged our clothes,
small hands pulling two Gullivers
toward the fire. The music stopped.

Stranded hitchhiking,
I said, and glad to hear music.

Our cigarettes welcome,
we were handed mugs of strong tea.

The woman sang again
and the men watchfully accompanied her,
the children wandered off, leaving my school friend
and me wishing that we had been raised like them.

Between her songs, on wood steps to
a flower-painted caravan,
the woman told us only the old and young
were here, the rest were in town and would be back
      when the pubs closed.

We knew what she meant: we need to
      get out of here before
      the real world intrudes.

AT MOLL'S GAP, IN KERRY

People hurry out the door
I see them through the window

holding up their cameras
video recorders phones

something I have seen before
in presence of tragedy

get a shot of what's happened
forget to extend a hand

once outside the door I am
hit by a monster rainbow

SUMMER AFTERNOON IN KERRY

The clouds rolled over the
Macgillicuddy Reeks,
the downpours were sudden,
heavy and frequent.

At the town bridge in Sneem
an Englishwoman said
the driver abandoned
their structured bus tour and
now he drove while it rained
and stopped when the rain stopped
regardless of where.

She said an old woman
at a roadside cottage
seemed quite pleased when the bus
stopped and fifty people
or so poured out and asked
to photograph her and
her climbing roses.

PEITREAL

Though I could not recall the Gaelic word
for petrol, I could say fill up my car,
if it is your will, which I said in a
natural way to the man at the pump
in the gaeltacht west of Macroom in Cork,
contributing what I could to the last
glimmers of Irish in everyday use.

Not speak Irish but I speak very good,
he said to me in a Polish accent,
not knowing that if he had responded
to me rapidly in his native tongue,
I would have assumed that he was speaking
the local dialect and retreated
to conquerors' imperial English.

5

SECURE WARD

He's not handcuffed to the bed
and the big policeman eating
dinner from a paper plate

pays no heed to him because
he is a vegetable.

They do not know if he will
ever regain consciousness.

Others talk about him as
if he was already dead.

A physical therapist,
not much older than he is,
explains what she does for him

to his mother, who listens
impassively, suggesting
she may have seen worse than this.

His younger brother hangs back
and slyly leaves a get-well
card on the bedside table.

The therapist notices
the penciled words in the card:
Wake up, you lazy fucker.

Looking at his open eyes
that are nonresponding, she
says the words softly to him.

TROPHIES

In the club that morning they notice all
the silver cups and plates have been stolen.

The competition golf is due to start
that afternoon. Then someone notices

half a figure on the tidal mudflats
among the heedless searching water birds,

head and shoulders and arms above the mud.
His right hand clutches the neck of a sack.

His pleas for help, his prayers, finally
screams go unheard among the cries and calls

of gulls and the long-legged wading birds
that feed nocturnally between the tides.

A priest says his holding on to the sack
could have been an act of restitution.

Some say they know that he refused to quit,
even as the water crept up his face.

You can see I was not wasting my time.
Loosen my grip on the sack. Open it.

SILENCING THE MAN WHO
KNEW MORE THAN ANYONE

They tell a story of Mahaffy,
Dublin University provost
about a hundred years ago.

It was then the custom for fellows
to remain at table till the signal
was given that dinner was over
by the provost's getting to his feet.

No matter what they talked about,
Mahaffy knew more than anyone
and aired his ideas at length
before rising from the table.

In order to silence him, some fellows
quietly arranged to talk of a thing
about which Mahaffy knew nothing.

But what? A fellow took a volume
of the very recently published
Encyclopedia Britannica's

nineteen eleven edition
and let it fall open at random:
to a page on Chinese music.

Each fellow was assigned some text
and talking points were chosen to extend
through dinner and silence Mahaffy.

They talked and Mahaffy was silent,
causing them to smile among themselves.

When finally Mahaffy stood
he glowered at them and spoke at last:

Gentlemen, it seems you have enjoyed
that article on Chinese music –
you should know it was I who wrote it.

DUBLIN BUS STOP

Miss Browne, an elderly gentlewoman,
waited midway between Chapelizod
and Islandbridge, alongside Phoenix Park,
for buses, the drivers of which she knew
enjoyed speeding along this empty stretch.

When a speeding green doubledecker bus
entered her field of vision, despite her
small size, advanced years and poor sight, she leaped
into its path, waving her arms, basket
and umbrella, loudly calling, Ahoy!

A friend heard one driver ask another
if he knew her name or her dwelling place –
they talked of her as ancient sailors talked
on shore of the dangers beyond belief
that rise from the mythological deeps.

ANOTHER DUBLIN BUS STOP

Near Heuston station
she saw a man wave
at buses, clueless
in accepted ways
of how to catch one.

His clothes were oddly
put together and
out of style but clean.

She could only wish
more homeless people
were as clean as this.

He was handsome and
she charitable.

He politely asked
her to drop him off
at an old fashioned
conservative club.

There she declined to
join him for a drink.

MONK

You old-timers may still remember
the tonsured monk in a brown habit
who begged for alms on the winter streets

in brightly colored hand-knitted socks
and sandaled feet and who liked to say,
Saint Francis never got to Dublin

PRAYER FOR NIALL A.

May he be at peace
in the great beyond
where old time heroes
lift their drinks and talk
and the clouds are made
of cigarette smoke
with harp music loud
and angels dancing

DEAN'S GRANGE

I walked with her among the stones
where family and friends are laid
and she remembered this one here
and that one there and pointing said
she was quite a tennis player,
of which the devout inscription
on the tombstone made no mention

NOT LOST

It is All Souls' Eve, daylight nearly gone,
the dead are free to roam and visit us
who go beyond the safety of home.

We walk together where we always walk
and talk about the things we always talk.

I hear my walking crush the fallen leaves
and see the leaves beside me hardly stir
beneath the gesture of her weightless feet.

6

LORD OF THE YARD

Body feathers erectile,
his tail feathers exploded
into a vertical fan
that formed an aureole of threat
around his avian body,
reptilian eyes,
dinosaur talons,
pulsing red and blue wattles,
he screamed a war cry and charged.

I ran as hard
as an eight-year-old can run
and cleared the chicken wire fence,
looked back and then

watched him shrink to a turkey
strutting its turf.

PLOWSHARES INTO SWORDS

At eight or nine, with a steel nib on a shaft of wood
that I dipped in the ceramic inkwell in my desk,
      I practiced penmanship.

We fought in the yard and punctured each other with nibs,
and this came to the reluctant attention of our
      scholarly headmaster.

Sometimes bewildered, at times amused, often alarmed,
looking up from deep in the classics, I think he saw
      a barbarian horde.

DUBLIN HALLOWEEN LONG GONE

A spool of black thread was payed out from door to hiding place
and one end was tied to a heavy brass doorknocker.

> The doorknocker
> knocked on the door.
> The door opened

and the householder stood in a rectangle of light
looking out at the empty night in which unquiet souls
roamed as ghosts on neighborhood streets where once they walked.

> When the door closed,
> the thread was pulled,
> doorknocker knocked

and the door opened again to the souls who find no rest.
Few people broke the thread, although it never occurred to us
they might be playing a game they themselves remembered playing.

> An old fellow
> none of us liked
> hit one of us.
>
> We leaned a plank
> against his door
> and rang the bell.

The door whipped open, the plank hit his forehead and
we saw how he lay beneath the plank, dead on the floor.

One of us knew what to do: we went half a mile away and
ostentatiously identified ourselves to kids we knew.
On my way home later that night I looked and saw

> no ambulance
> or police cars
> outside his door.

Next morning he stood uninjured waiting for the bus,
revived perhaps by the prayers of wandering souls.

WARRIOR, AGE THIRTEEN

Before you throw someone over your shoulder
or disarm a knife-wielding attacker, you
        have to learn
        how to fall.

I think they must have meant some kind of futon
or at most a low to the floor modern bed,
not a wheeled Victorian cast iron bed
like mine, higher than a dining room table,
but I did not know this and stood on its edge,
focused my mind, relaxed my muscles and fell
        backward full
        length floorward.

The sudden crashes and subsequent whimpers
unnerved my aunt a floor beneath. I explained
about Japanese martial arts, a concept
new to her and one she could not understand.
She thought a priest might know, and I think he said
the Japanese were pagans, what could you do.

CHANT

You hear versions of Gregorian chant
rendered by university scholars
that could flake the tonsures of drowsy monks

gathered in a church as cold as a grave
before streaks of day can tint the stained glass,
men who tried to be humble and simple.

A priest in school said Gregorian chant
was made for men who did not imagine
and who found it hard to see God in things.

He conscripted a choir of twenty boys,
taking all our class of fourteen-year-olds
without any test as to who could sing.

I sang along with everyone, holding
a page of familiar Latin words
and square notation on a four-line staff.

A tone was allowed for each syllable
of text, the tones arranged in groups of four –
the kind of chant preferred by raucous monks

before a day among the cabbages
and beehives and texts to be copied, with
none of the musical complications

urged by Odo of Cluny or Jerome
of Moravia. We were terrible.

The priest saw gain in this for his belief
that religious medieval people
were more advanced than people are today.

We did not improve and the choir expired.

The priest moved on to new failures but kept
hopes for chant alive and smiled to recall

another teacher's pretended surprise
that he was leading us in choral work
of an atonal German composer.

BLUE-WINGED OLIVE

Dimpled the water top
as if it had six feet.
A trout swallowed the hook.

Once I caught a trout
on an awkwardly
home-tied olive fly

to a friend's envy.
Just look at its face!
He pointed. I looked.

A tranquil face.
It's retarded,
he claimed – for it

to take such a fly,
this could only be
a handicapped fish.

Other Places

WARRIOR

I must have been sixteen,
fresh off the Dublin boat,
in Macclesfield, south of
Manchester, hitchhiking
south to London, at two
in the morning, beneath
the red brick wall of a
lunatic asylum,
swallowing beer from a
glass imperial quart,
when I took a notion
to throw the empty
over the asylum wall
and headlights caught me
in the act of throwing and
my two friends cursed me
as they thumbed a ride,
when, to our surprise,
the car stopped and we
assured the driver
we would behave, and he,
a Yank sergeant,
uniform and cropped hair,
said he didn't give
a damn, he would kill
all three of us if
we tried anything,
he had been up since five
the previous day
and was nodding off
at the wheel and we
looked Irish and we
liked to talk and he
needed talk to stay
awake

COUNTRY LIFE

Victorian sideburns
headmaster's nose
and inscrutable eye
the hawk detects movement.

What might have moved?
Birds could be picked by hand
motionless in the thorns.

Insects conduct
their three-hour-flightlife
aerial orgies
over the pond.

Radar eyeballs a frog
green as a lily pad
can't hold its darting tongue.

Grass moves and flicks aside
and stands upright again —
a creature advancing.

Hawk dives and lifts
a snake in its talons
flaps out of view.

The frog hops
nearer to the flies
and one by one
the birds take up their calls.

A SHARD IN SOMERSET

Near the Somerset village Timberscombe
on a right of way across rising fields
I picked a shard from a new-plowed furrow,
a cloverleaf, blue on a white background
webbed in cracks, and a pale green stem attached
to part of a blood-red petal or fruit,
too rude in craft for large-scale industry.

A dealer would know the shard's origin:
a Roman villa, tiled and mosaicked,
beneath this unimaginative farm,
or bowl of a Celtic monk, the trefoil
piously depicting the Trinity,
or tall Parliament fellows with blue coats
and badges and long basket-hilt swords here
caught a hiding monarchist unaware
while eating his dish of honeyed gruel,
or dinner plate forgot and trodden by
a ponderous yeoman chewing a straw,
or a wicked rakehell's who boxed the ears
of the pretty dairymaid's brat, his son,
when the lad dropped a jug of hop-brewed ale.

In England's damp and well aerated soil
blades of bronze and iron have bloomed in rust,
their wielders and their victims turned to dust,
and relic hunters must expect to find
more broken teacups than stone arrowheads.

ST. IVES

In May, before the summer crowd,
the two of us, lying on sand,
the rocky end of Porthminster,
she, oiled and tanning, fast asleep,
my reading eyes bothered by glare
on the page, a submarine breaks
the glittering surface and floats
without any further movement
only a hundred yards away,
a jet fighter swoops, with its roar
trailing behind, they meet and kiss,
and the sub then eases beneath –
I will not tell her when she wakes
and thinks she knows what drives my mind:
male military fantasy
to spoil a cozy afternoon

WHISPERING LEAVES

Prince Charles is known
to stop and talk
when quite alone
on garden walks.

The humble bean,
loyal spinach,
repay in green
his patronage.

Since British sprouts
may talk and hear
and plant their doubts
in royal ears,

politicos
from Ulster freed
his potatoes
for orange trees.

AT A FENCE

A poet looks through a bramble ditch
at grass in multitudinous greens,
notes the barbs on rusted strands of wire
taut among the blackberry flowers
and remembers, too, the thorns on stems.

Over that fence, an entrepreneur
sees in grass an opportunity,
foundations deeply excavated,
to build to last a thing that's solid
and of benefit to humankind.

I watch ivy climb its ruined walls.

THEIR NEW HOUSE

She is the one at home,
he says, I am away
at work all day and I
travel so much, I've left
the choice of our new house
completely up to her.

That is how he sees it,
she says, yet when I found
an old place with lots of
tiny rooms that I could
fix up, each differently,

This is too dark, he said,
we could never live here.

PATRICIA

She went, she said,
because it was
beside the sea.

The others went
because it was
a navy town.

AT AN EARLY HOUR

What a joy it is for her on cold mornings
to lie in bed and listen to the radio,
especially those BBC nature programs

on which people named Trevor and Nigel
tramp the frosty woods and fields in search
of living things abroad at such an hour.

    She can hear some of them,
particularly birds, songbirds that sing
in unexpected places at inappropriate times.

But it is not all honeysuckle for Trevor and Nigel:
the wind is from Finisterre and Tuskar,
        it is cold, there is mud.

        When mud slurps on Nigel
    or when Trevor falls
    audibly her boyfriend

    beside her in her warm bed
    who hates Trevor and Nigel
    has been known to smile.

WINNER

        The thoroughbred
Denman, after winning the Hennessy Gold Cup
for the second time, being led on the green turf
before a cheering Newbury crowd that has bet
on the winning favorite, beneath the jockey
smiling and waving his whip, the trainer in tears,
        the thoroughbred
has eyes only for the red-shirted stable girl
        who pats his neck
and whispers to him what a good boy he has been

GHOSTLY FOOTSTEPS IN LONDON

The painter Michael Rogan in his early years,
handed the key to a haunted flat, was told
perhaps an artist like himself would not share the fears
of others for things that make the blood run cold.

Having dossed in flats with crazed, sane and bent
and used an empty glasshouse as a studio,
for lots of space at minimal rent
Michael was willing to risk a ghost or two.

Or so he thought, but on the very first night
when Michael backed to view a canvas on the easel
his breath grew short and his heart pounded in fright
as nothing walked past his nose on its way to hell.

Walk it did and wore shoes, and the noise of its steps
across the middle of the room and through a wall
told him this had been a woman once, now only steps —
without scent, rustle, warmth   nothing else at all.

He knew her walk and as he came to know the times
she passed through the room, his fear of her subsided —
of other beings too, who were regular as chimes
of whatever clock the otherworld provided.

Two pairs of children's feet skipped across the floor,
perhaps two sisters, always in a hurry.
And showing all was not whole on the opposite shore,
a man's uneven tread, a limp, heavy with worry.

Michael warned his living visitors
about his visitants and tried to calm their panic
at the fast-moving, darting footsteps of the sisters,
disembodied but palpably sonic.

Although no footsteps came when the hour was late
his friends by then had long since fled,
and although the amount of work he did was great
his big complaint was his unshared bed.

One day he saw a pair of girls walking down the street
and noticed something peculiar
in the sound they made with their feet,
indefinite yet somehow familiar.

Their feet, incarnate in the afternoon air,
on a flagstone passageway beside the building
where he lived, transmitted, perhaps through metal buried there,
with ghost fidelity a fleshless walking.

Later, behind him, near the bank, he heard her sound
or one exactly like the one that crossed his room
into the wall — and decided, turning around,
to meet the woman from beyond the tomb.

BLUES AND ROYALS

A mounted policeman rides in front,
halting cars near Hyde Park Corner.

The horsemen ride two by two
in dark cloaks on dark horses.

Their silver helmets have red streamers
and each holds a sword, the blade upright.

They cut across the traffic lanes,
looking neither to right nor left.

They move like things from another world:
ghosts at midday on a city street.

If they pace through the side of a bus
will they emerge from its other side?

CEREMONIAL DUTY

On duty, a soldier of the Foot Guards
stood outside the building, his eyes open
beneath a bearskin, ignoring tourists
and cameras, seemingly unbreathing.

A woman posed on either side, a third
held a camera, and all three pleaded
with their man to join them for the photo.

About the soldier's age, he shrugged and said,
I'm sorry, mate, to do this thing to you.

A suggestion of a smile just flickered
along the facial immobility.

BROMPTON CEMETERY

Large angels are few,
as are lifesize statues
of despairing women.

Solitary men
take the accustomed place
of angels and women.

Do the living give
the dead the notion they
have not been forgotten?

HIGHGATE CEMETERY

George Eliot was here before Karl Marx
but his giant head is the biggest stone
and when you look at other stones you see
how socialists and communists who sought
twentieth century London refuge
having had their people politics crushed
nestle in earth beds around their thinker
himself a philosopher in exile

NOORDOOSTPOLDER

Now far inland
in drained Holland
once Zuider Zee
then IJsselmeer
the village pier
extends on stilts
beneath which heaves
a sea of leaves

NORSK FOTO

In the eerie light of an
old photograph in Norway
a young man in silhouette
stands next to a gas street lamp
viewing a ship at anchor,
its tall masts hanging with lines.

Impossible to decide
whether he's a trapped local
passively summoning up
a Tahiti in his mind
or Atlantic-tossed orphan
who has paused to rest his soul
before its creaking prison.

THUNDER OUTSIDE MOSCOW

Thunder tips his hat like Pasternak's father
and takes photographs, blinding us with flashes,
exposing things that hide in plain sight, etching
in unfamiliar ways, making us blink,
clad in Russia's thick coat of dark conifers
among the blowsy Czarist meadow flowers

THIS WAY OUT

Of four Hungarians
escaping the Nazis,
one stole a map, although
its labels meant nothing
to these Hungarians,
of alpine routes through
Austria to Switzerland
by which they could escape.

Dazed, half-starved, near frozen,
they came to Switzerland
and showed the map they used
escaping the Nazis
to a Swiss official,
who indicated one
particular: the map
displayed the Pyrenees.

BEASTS
(*after Jean Perret*)

Quit the howling
               out there in the dark
     whatever you are.
               Can't you scent us?
     We men are here.
Beasts, keep quiet and
     keep together,
or else:
               Civilization
               will build you
a zoological park,
               a garden of adjustment.

LIZARD KING

A black cat slinks between the tombs. Jim lives.
The funereal shade of evergreens,
mist, furred moss, ground creeper and moist clipped yew,
raked gravel paths, dry fountains, weathered stone,
a trunk grotesquely twisted, gnarled, the shape
of the body on which its roots have fed.

Columned temples, bronze mourners large as life,
the pomp and circumstance surrounding death
in nineteenth century France's glory,
the imagined peace of a world beyond.
The black cat slips between the graves. Jim lives.

A marshal skilled in colonial wars,
a famed composer of grand opera,
a tomb decorated with skulls and bats.
A marble angel weeps. This way to Jim.

Flowers stuck in bottles, labels attached.
The black cat blinks its yellow eyes. Jim's here.

THE FOREST AT NIGHT

Not far from where a sleeping hitchhiker
had been discovered in the woods a month
ago, mutilated the police said,
attacked by wolves a local farmer claimed
although the last wolf in this part of France
had been hunted down in his grandfather's
time, shivering cold in my sleeping bag
beneath a rustling canopy of leaves
on the first cold night of mid October,
I saw pairs of shining eyes around me
warily darting sideways and moving
nearer and I jumped up with my knife and
squeaking they scattered on the woodland floor

AROMA

Anthony Barton remembered
on one occasion
having to make impromptu comments
on some of his own vintages
in front of visiting wine writers.

Suddenly my vocabulary
dried up, he recalled.

I was gazing out the window
and declared the first thing I saw.
Roses, I announced.

Dutifully they wrote *roses*.

Then I had another sniff
and, strangely enough,
the sample reeked of roses.

CRUSADER

Well, here you are
setting out on the Second Crusade
      and you get word
you can't bring any falcons or hounds,
any concubines or troubadours.

      Raise up your glaive
and canter east with the oriflamme.

ARLES PARKING GARAGE

You could see how someone raised
in the thin tormented streets
of medieval Arles
might design this garage's
tight concrete passageways and
the little elbowroom for
a troubadour or driver
to slide in a crevice in
the aboveground burial
your automobile achieves

SNAILS

Snails believe in architects.

They crawl on moistened concrete,
grind their bellies on grit and
secrete locomotive slime.

They genuinely prefer
this to natural fiber.

Sit and think how very slow
mobile-home land mollusks go.

THINK OF FLOWERS

      Think of flowers
as tiny multiple explosions in a Dutchman's brain
      before their colors
bleed in livid streaks across lamplit interiors

      Almond blossoms
attract Ibiza bees in February
as spring creeps northward out of Africa
      wind moans in Holland

ISLAND

Before daylight
mounts the hillside
the roosters crow,
the hoopoe makes
its liquid calls,
and I wonder
if what I guessed
can be the truth,
lying awake,
alone, silent

SKETCHES OF SPAIN IN THE 1950s

1
(*for Charles Reece*)

In a dusty town, in Catalan hills,
the urchins played a game barefoot,

the boys in ragged hand-me-downs,
girls in tattered local costume.

They stopped the game, wide-eyed, silent,
to watch the painter open up his paints.

His grammar careful and his accent strange,
he asked for a glass of water.

All the children — seven or eight —
ran inside a nearby doorway.

A girl returned and handed him
a glass brimming with cool white wine.

He smiled and pointed to his paints
and said they were watercolors.

The girl said it was regarded
an insult to serve water in these hills.

She ran inside the house once more.
He rested where a wall cast shade.

The children came out one by one
in Sunday clothes, their faces washed, hair combed.

They stood before him in a line
in diminishing height from left to right.

Their mother, enclosed in a fancy shawl,
emerged, nodded and took her place.

After a pause, with gentle dignity,
in an ancient suit and paperwhite shirt,

the master of the house appeared,
shook the painter's hand, joined his wife

behind the line of serious children,
no longer picturesque ragamuffins.

The painter dipped his brush tip in the wine,
held the paper, began to paint.

2
(*for Wilhelmina Barns-Graham*)

No young Scotsmen had ever misbehaved
when she had drawn abstract shapes of boulders
half sunk and smooth as whale backs in the moors.

Here the rock was warm as flesh and its scales
glistened in the sun, and here a young man —
it seemed a different one each time — lay down

and posed for her, and if she turned to draw
another rock he rose and lay on that.
She tried to draw the rock without the man.

She could not draw the rock without the man
and so she put him in and made his shape
abstract, deeply insulting each of them.

One man lingered to gaze at a drawing
over her shoulder, and with her pencil
she rapped his knuckles when he stroked her arm.

HOME FURNISHINGS

Two couches and three armchairs arranged on sand
in an empty but intimate quadrangle
on the morning beach at Barceloneta
suggest transients with nocturnal humor

DINING OUT

An Indian restaurant in Lisbon, too spicy for me?
        Waiting for food to come,
I see before me a small ceramic object.
Cuplike, it is empty and too small to drink from.
It has indecipherable decorations.
I examine it in an unobtrusive way.
The waitress takes the object and brings another.
        It is filled with toothpicks.
Obrigado, I say, one of my Portuguese words.

AFTER FERNANDO PESSOA

1
Steeples, the only things that I can see
above the trees, mark the locations of
the valley settlements. The steeples point
heavenward for spiritual people.

I would like to climb inside a steeple.
The door is locked. Do not walk on the grass.
The steeple, although in good condition,
is merely a thing of stone and timber.

You can be happy in Australia
for as long as you do not go there.

2
When you open the window
you see the fields and river
but are they what you perceive?

If you open your eyes you
can see the trees and flowers –
see *them* or just ideas?

When you open the window
what you see are dreams and fears,
never what is really there.

3
They may be speaking Hindi or Tamil
outside my window as I write these words
and they point the bricks of the old building,
deriving a certain satisfaction
no doubt from level lines and fixed patterns,
which is not how I lay my words in rows.

There's one thing we share in the work we do:
we stand on boards suspended by thin ropes.

4
My being shattered like an empty vase
released from the hands of a careless maid,
breaking into more pieces than made up
the material substance of the vase.

That may not be physically possible
but I felt I had more awareness now
than in my existence as a whole vase.

My fall sounded like a shattering vase
and celestial beings looked over
the stair rail to see what the maid had dropped.

They did not grow angry at her, instead
they were forgiving when they realized
the empty vase was of little value.

They looked down at the shards that seemed to be
unconscious of celestial beings
and smiled at the careless maid, who then cleaned
but missed a fragment, its shiny side up,

which gleamed and caused celestial beings
to wonder later what it was down there.

AFTER MARTIAL

I:LXIV
She is young, beautiful and rich
and people say that she can act,
yes, but when she extends long legs
on a show and raises her chin
to tell us how hard she works to
help humanity she loses
youth, beauty and hopefully some
of her future earning power

III:XXVI
Although he lets us know he owns
the roof above our heads, the pool
in which we float, the alcohol
in which we float, money enough
to make us flail out of our depth,
we all have a stake in his wife

V:LIX
In bringing a bottle of wine
of moderate price, I do you
a favor. Your burden will be
lightened when you come to my house.

VIII:LXI
He does not hide he wishes harm
to me because I can afford
a summer house in the Hamptons,
envious and unaware that
anxieties accompany
a summer house in the Hamptons

VIII:LXXVI
Tell me the truth, he likes to say,
the truth is what I want to hear.
Very well, then, tell him the truth:
truth is not what he wants to hear.

IX:LXXXI
A poet says my poems are
not polished. I prepare dishes
to please my guests, not fellow cooks.

X:XII
I will miss her while she is gone
a winter month in island sun
and look forward to her return
when in just a matter of days
among pale friends she will forget
her lazy frolics on the beach

XII·XXX
You hear he is clean and sober,
a quality that recommends
a man for hire but not a friend

XII:LXI
He need not fear that I will write
a poem that makes fun of him
because lions are not hostile
to butterflies. He needs to fear
the ones who write on bathroom walls.

XIII:VII
If you have beans to bubble
in a red earthenware pot
you can politely decline
any sumptuous dinner

AT NIGHT IN AREZZO

Becoming too warm, I wake and cast aside the goose down quilt
which falls double on the woman who is dreaming at my side.

On waking, she feels rivulets of sweat branching on her skin
and believes that mosquitoes have given her malaria.

We are sleeping, we are dreaming in the rose and saffron tent.

PELOPONNESE

1
Beneath the top
of a wind-scoured cliff
at Mount Parnon
four nuns maintain
Moni Elonis.

Somewhere on the rock
a raven barks,
a devil's snicker.

2
The small freighter
sailed for Russia
from Githio.

In dock water
oranges bob.

3
Germans using up the water
      to wash themselves,
and Greeks breaking up the mountains
      to build churches,
what will become of the place?

Look at all the evidence
of previous disasters.

4
In Old Kardamili
a goat bleats
in the olive trees
and tinkles its bell.

BLUE

Blue! Blue! You must all dress in blue,
whatever you have that is blue,
no matter what shade.

The Mediterranean sea
and the sky above it are blue,
although different shades.

Shaking in grass on the cliff top,
the petals of wild plants are blue,
a delicate shade.

I ask a knot of old locals,
You like blue? They lie by a rock
and gaze from its shade.

Blue is a color for crazies,
a woman shouts back.

Themselves
               they drape
                             in black,
and we stand
               on their land.

IN CRETE

When tourists ask him why
there are no fish to eat
at the harbor café
the owner frowns and says:

In Crete we fish at night
and the fish are asleep.

DESERT HOMECOMING

A woman in black shrouds
threw her arms around him,
wailed, the ululation
of her voice rose and fell
as she hugged him closer,
a melodious voice,
its high wavering notes
moved with shades of feeling —
sound that raised the hair on skin
before we thought of music

No Willows

AN OLD STORY

A woman carried uphill
to her stone abode
on a winding narrow path

two pots of water balanced
on a bamboo pole.
Every morning, a neighbor

said, I notice that one pot
is cracked and leaks what
seems like a lot of water.

It loses more than a third
of what it contains,
the woman said and ran her

fingertips along the crack.
Why don't you fix it
or make yourself another?

The woman shouldered the pole
and balanced the pots,
hanging brimful with water.

She gestured to the uphill
winding narrow path
and began her daily climb.

Unsure, the neighbor followed.
The leaking pot dripped
and dripped along the left side

of the winding narrow path.
In a damp thin band
grew abundant wildflowers.

The other side was dusty
and dry. The neighbor
smiled then and went no farther.

NO PLUM BLOSSOMS

AFTER AN OLD POEM

Near the East Gate
the young women
pass like the clouds
pass in the sky.
      My thoughts of them
      soon drift away.

            Look at that one –
            her hands, her eyes,
            the way she moves.

Near the town wall
the soft-skinned girls
sway like the reeds
sway on the lake.
      Glance a moment
      and move along.

            This one's demure –
            pretending not
            to see me stare.

AFTER ANOTHER OLD POEM

She lies on her bed and she cannot sleep.

Through the window the moon looks in at her.

Gently drifting off, she dreams a man calls
to her and without thinking answers yes.

AFTER HSIN CH`I-CHI

Hardly a line on my face,
I talked about broken hearts
and the cruel ways of love.

Now that sorrow has seeped through
my skin, I pick words like these:
Nice day for the time of year.

AFTER CHAO I

Before sleep, I thought up
a line that resounded.
Not trusting memory,
I rose to write it on paper.

Awoken, my wife smiled
indulgently. She said,
If only we could get
the kids to do that with schoolwork.

AFTER SU TUNG-P`O

They gather around the baby and say,
Look at him smile – he's so good-natured and
 so intelligent.

I'd prefer him obstinate and greedy.
I want my son to enjoy, unlike me,
 success in the world.

AFTER YUAN CHEN AND CONRAD AIKEN

You married for love. One by one,
your golden rings and ornaments
were pawned by me for casks of wine.
We lived on soup of roadside herbs.

All I can give you, now I'm rich,
are blossoms for your marble stone.

We had no superstition we
would meet again another place,
although we planned to side by side
lie in the darkness of our tomb.

I wait around and long for you,
at night I see your anxious face.

BROTHERS

When Ts`ao P`i became emperor he appointed
his brother Chih to a succession of
distant minor posts.

AFTER TS`AO P`I

Look at that isolated cloud,
what does its shape remind you of?

You will have to be quick, the winds
tear it apart before our eyes.

I'd say its shape reminds you of
someone homeless, a frightened man.

AFTER TS`AO CHIH

Far from my native roots
I roll, a tumbleweed,
without rest or relaxation

along the seven paths,
beyond eleven roads,

dropped in gorges and
lifted by whirlwinds,

gliding, sliding,
find no handhold,

floating, rambling,
no fixed abode,

I envy prairie grass
that burns in wildfire flames
and drops its ash upon its roots

HOMECOMING FROM WAR
(after Tu Fu)

I travel by night
and the winter moon
shines on the white bones
that lie on what was
once a battlefield.

Men I meet by day
move with groans and sobs,
most of them wounded,
some even bleeding.

Gifts for my thin wife,
her face is aglow,
my little son, pale,
dirty, without socks,
turns his back and weeps.

My two small daughters
wear tattered and patched
clothing (on one patch
the water spirit
appears upside down)

and having survived
war with the rebels,
I submit to wild
questioning as they
fight to pull my beard.

When darkness returns
we burn candles and
look at each other
as if in a dream.

NO CHRYSANTHEMUMS

AFTER YUAN MEI

The oak feels the icy breeze,
knows the end of summer nears,
now is whispering the news,
each to each, among its leaves

AFTER HAN YU

Monkeys playing in the branches
      see their reflections
in lake water and when ripples
      distort images
they yelp in fear and look behind
      to see what threatens

AFTER P`I JIH-HSIU

These hungry ignorant mosquitoes drink
the blood of hungry ignorant people.
Easy, because they lack protective screens.

If insects had more imagination,
the mosquitoes could feed upon the blood
of sleek people reclining on clean sheets.

AFTER FAN CH`ENG-TA

Farmers celebrate a good harvest
and thank the spirits who blessed the land.

Invited spirits who come will see
the men legless and the women dance.

AFTER YUAN MEI

Seventy-seven years old, yes sir, and here I am again
after I said my final goodbye to you just three years gone,
here I am, expecting chicken and wine and celebration.

I said that was my farewell, you would never see me again
and you don't know how bad it makes me feel to cheat you again.

AFTER POETS OF THE LATE T`ANG

TONIGHT

Your mother did it when she was young,
the moon lit her tears and little smile.

You will smell the pine,
                            your skin on mine,
and hear the cries of tall walking birds

and safe together inside my car
we can watch the mountain goblins feed.

APART

Down there and up here the winter
snow and wind keep us flights apart.

Although you have little interest
in the Packers and the Steelers,

separately let's watch the game
early Sunday evening.
                        Then we

can phone and you can say what you
think of Superbowl Forty-Five.

LONGING

The big trucks creep uphill, nose to tail,
out of sight, with brand names and messages.

Machines know my name and email me.

Sometimes a face or something said
on television reminds me of you.

Nothing on Facebook, nothing on Twitter.

I think you may have lost or forgotten
my telephone number.
                      Now is when

I wonder where you are this moment.

LOST

I heard you say that the caged bird owes no allegiance,
that the wind-tossed flower may soon be lost by the tree.

I'm ashamed to think I was not always kind to you.
No one knows where you are,
                                only the bright watching moon.

NO WILLOWS

AFTER MENG CHIAO

      My bike has a punctured tire
from a stone or root on this mountain trail.
      Night falls and I hear wolves howl.
Breathe slow, my heart is a fluttering flag.

AFTER MA CHIH-YUAN

If Mayor Bloomberg telephones,
or Hillary Clinton, even
if President Obama calls,
say this unshaven citizen
is not drunk yet and cannot speak

AFTER CH`IAO CHI

Nevada
casino

the body
playing here

and the soul
not yet dead